Keep It Simple, Stupid

Secrets of Face-to-Face Selling

By
William J. Montgomery

PublishAmerica
Baltimore

First printing

ISBN: 1-4137-0587-1
PUBLISHED BY PUBLISHAMERICA, LLLP
www.publishamerica.com
Baltimore

Printed in the United States of America

This book is dedicated to my entire family, with special thanks to Penny for her support and encouragement, and finally to hugh, who showed me what true courage and determination really is.

Selling in my own opinion is a craft, something that is rarely mastered overnight, but like most crafts requires a good teacher and practice. I was once, just like you are now, looking for a way to improve my chances of succeeding in direct sales and looking for the answers to my many questions in a book which, unlike you, I was never fortunate enough to find.

True — there may be some very good books on the market about selling, but in my own opinion they are too long winded and tend to give the reader an immediate impression that selling requires a master's degree in psychology and communications. Nothing could be further from the truth; the large majority of successful salespeople had no previous sales experience, nor qualifications in selling skills.

I personally try to look upon my craft as I would a game and like most games it has an objective that has to be reached before you can win or progress to the next level. You just need to know the rules and what tactics to use in the game in order to win — "getting that sale."

Selling isn't as complicated a matter as one might think and the very fact you are reading this book tells me that you either want to start a career in selling or improve your existing sales performance — believe me when I say you will.

I'm going to reveal little-known tactics to you that may shock, or at the very least surprise you about direct selling, plus all you need to know to create a sales script, get into their homes/offices, get their attention, get them to believe in you and your product, and ultimately get that sale.

Firstly, I will assume that you, the reader, have little or no direct selling experience and as such I will do my best to keep to the KISS theory, "**Keep It Simple, Stupid**"— something all good salespeople try and adhere to when selling. No doubt you've heard it mentioned somewhere.

This is the only real acronym I will use in my book; too many are used in sales and are, in my own opinion, using my own acronym, ATWOT — "a total waste of time"!

Selling, as you probably know, is creating a need, want and desire for the product or service you have to offer to the end user, whom I refer to throughout this book as "the prospect." You, as the salesperson, have to convince someone verbally to believe in you, your product and part with their hard-earned cash to buy your product or service. Not an easy task given the fact that chances are they have survived without your product or service up until now. It really does help your position as the salesperson if you genuinely believe in your product or service and can be naturally enthusiastic; if you aren't, and you are unable to feign it to a very high standard — move on.

Being in direct sales has its own unique challenges, unlike the retail or car salesperson whose prospective customers have already expressed a desire, need or want simply by physically visiting their store or showroom; you have to create that need starting from scratch. There you are, face to face with someone you know nothing about, and you're intending to leave them with something they had, until now, perhaps never even needed or wanted, and, best of all, they have to pay you for it.

Remember, too, that people hate to be "sold to," don't they? What happens when you visit a store and the assistant asks you "Do you need any help?" We usually respond by saying "No thanks, I'm just looking," as we don't want to be pressured or persuaded into buying.

Therefore, it's important to think like a "buyer" before you begin selling.

Walk in Their Shoes

Before you can make that sale, you have to understand how your typical prospect thinks.

Imagine for a moment what it must be like from the prospect's point of view.

They have just came home from a terrible day at work and simply want peace and quiet. They have just started to relax for the evening, enjoying a nice glass of wine perhaps, and suddenly the front door is knocked or the door bell is rung. Naturally, they ask themselves who it could possibly be? They weren't expecting anyone.

They now have to get up from that nice, comfy sofa, and walk to the door still wondering who is disturbing their peace, their quality time. They open the door slightly and, as they do so, peek around the door at who is there. Lo and behold, it's you in a nicely pressed suit wearing a big cheesy smile. They instantly scan you from head to toe and now know they don't know you, so you must be a salesperson; who else would be at their door at 7 p.m.?

They become even more guarded now, as they know you're going to try and sell them something they don't need or want and they are in no mood to listen. Their favorite TV show is just about to start, which doesn't help your position any, and they are just waiting for you to confirm their initial suspicions by introducing yourself and starting your sales pitch.

In the split seconds that this process took, the prospect has already made up excuses in their head for not wanting to listen or talk to you, and before you can start your sales pitch they say, "Sorry, I just don't have the time" or some other lame excuse and close the door in your face. You're left standing there with your mouth half open, stopped in mid-sentence, and once again you are looking at a closed door.

How many times have *you* done this sort of thing to a direct salesperson?

This example applies whether your prospect is at home or at work somewhere; their minds are generally on something else — be it the TV or the day's business tasks ahead of them.

It's very common in direct sales to have doors closed in your face; this is the harsh reality of direct selling. But don't despair; by the time you have read this entire book, you won't find yourself facing this situation very often, if indeed at all.

When people hear the terms "door to door" or "direct selling," they immediately conjure up an image of a man in an old brown suit carrying a large suitcase going door to door or office to office selling cleaning products, shower rings or whatever else the case may contain. Legend has it that all door-to-door salespeople wear one shoe bigger than the other, the larger one is used to get a foot in the doorway before it can be closed. In reality, nothing could be further from the truth. Direct salespeople more often than not represent respectable, large, household name companies, including major utility businesses and the financial services industry. Every business needs customers to survive and as such they each use different methods to attract them, including TV, radio, newspapers, telephone, direct mail; more often than not, direct sales representatives play a major role in most companies.

It's a Numbers Game.

Before you can sell you have to talk to people, as many as possible in fact. Time spent driving from location to location is wasted selling time. Don't try to fool yourself into thinking that the two-hour drive to see the potential customer can be classed as working; it isn't, it's wasted selling time.

Whenever possible, you should try to work within your own demographic area and minimize your traveling time. If you aren't talking to someone, you aren't selling, so make full use of your time. If you do have to travel far and wide, don't just travel 50 miles to see one client. Arrange a particular day to work that area, and if you are in business-to-business sales, get as many prior appointments as you can in that particular district, for that particular day. Remember, the more people you talk to the more sales you will ultimately achieve.

Selling really is a numbers game at the end of the day and here is one particular game that you can not only have some fun with, but also demonstrates to you how the sales process actually works.

The game is very easy to learn and can be great fun. After you've had some practice, try it out on your friends or colleagues, who will be totally baffled as to why you always win.

All you have to do is challenge someone to count to the number twenty (20) with you, and the person who gets to say the number twenty (20) wins. It doesn't really matter who goes first and the only rules to the game are that both you and your opponent can say no more than two numbers in succession in any one turn, and you must reply instantly. For example, assume you start *(you will never lose if you do)* by saying the number one (1), your opponent can then say number two (2) on his/her own or numbers two (2) and three (3). *No more than two numbers.* You can then respond by saying the numbers four (4) or the numbers four and five (4, 5) and so on. Whoever lands on number 20 first wins the game.

The way to win this particular game is by you simply staying one step ahead of your opponent by making sure that you land on the numbers 5, 8, 11, 14 and most importantly 17, which is the key number.

As long as you land on the number (17), you simply can't lose this game, as your opponent only has the choice of saying (18) or (18, 19), either way you win.

If you do start, say the numbers one (1) or (1,2). Your opponent can only say (2,3) or (3,4). You then say (5), they have to respond (6) or (6,7). You say (8), the opponent says (9) or (9, 10). You say (11) and as the game continues make sure you stop on numbers (14) and (17).

Using this tactic places you in complete control at all times and you are, in effect, manipulating the entire process. This game does a great job of actually showing what selling is all about, the numbers (5), (8), (11), and (14) are the questions in your script, and the number (17) is the close. Your opponent's answers are the replies to your scripted questions, which you easily overcome by simply staying one step ahead of the prospect by knowing what to say and when.

Your opponent, or in this case the prospect, not knowing the rules, simply won't think as you do and will simply say any old number(s) in response, without any real thought. Believe me when I tell you that they will be amazed as to how you keep winning. Go try it out!

Dress to Sell

Wearing the right clothes is very important when selling. Your appearance speaks volumes about you as a person, and people will make their minds up about you and your character within a few short seconds of meeting you. When you are meeting someone for the first time, it is very important to smile and be friendly. Be aware of your own body language and of your own tone of voice; speak and stand in a non-threatening manner at all times. Stay relaxed and be as friendly as you can; although you aren't there to make friends, it really will help you if the prospect takes a liking to you for the duration of your visit. When you are in the company of friends or family, you are usually relaxed; you won't go too far wrong if you simply *be yourself* in the company of a prospect. Don't be false by pretending to be someone that you aren't naturally; your prospect will see right through this, as would you.

TIP: If you are cold calling at someone's front door, don't be afraid to take a very small and deliberate step away from the prospect as they initially make eye contact with you after opening their front door. This lets them know that you are non-threatening, and it will actually assist you in relaxing them.

Let's assume for a moment that you are a door-to-door salesperson selling the new Super Dooper Pooper Scooper. This wonderful stick-like product will remove an animal's waste from your prospect's lawn in an instant, wrap the waste in biodegradable, nicely scented, hygienic plastic, and with the click of a button, will put it in the garbage. No more having to bend over with that local supermarket's plastic bag over your hand. It's a wonderful product, and, with the large number of pet owners out there, you have no end of potential customers to call upon.

So, how would you dress yourself to sell a pet feces collector?

Full business suit and tie; jeans and running shoes? True, you will be calling at any sort of address, from plush mansions to apartments; most people you know own a dog or cat, don't they?

Personally, I would always advise you to dress neutral when selling door to door. Clean black shoes *(everyone looks at your shoes and it's important to make sure they are clean and comfortable),* dark trousers, white- or light-colored shirt, and, yes, a tie. Nothing loud, keep it plain if you can and when it comes to selecting a jacket to wear, don't wear anything too expensive or flashy, dress down ever so slightly.

If I'm working in a plush neighborhood, I'd naturally keep my collar and tie nice and neat. For the not-so-plush neighborhoods, I loosen the tie a little and undo my top button or even roll up my shirt sleeves. Believe me when I say your appearance can make or break you in sales.

It's a very fine balancing act. In some neighborhoods, the last thing you want to do is walk around looking like a plain clothes police officer or some other government official — no one will open the door! Dress too flashy and you may end up being mugged!

I've heard direct salespeople complain how hardly anyone was at home in some streets, but once I'd pointed out that they were dressed like a detective or looked like a debt collector, the reason no one was apparently at home soon sets in.

Door-to-door sales is a totally different market from business-to-business sales, where a smart business suit is wholly appropriate, but it is still important to try and identify with your potential customers and dress accordingly. Bottom line: Try and dress to suit the customers and your product/service — not your own ego.

Gift of the Gab

I've often heard the expression that salespeople are born, not made, and I tend to disagree with this statement to a certain extent. Whilst it's true that some people do appear to have the "gift of the gab," most of us have the gift of speech, don't we? However, we also probably know someone who we would class as having "no personality" or "sense of humor," both of which are essential ingredients in any good direct salesperson. With the right training and support, I believe that most people can be **taught** how to sell and sell well — even those who have little or no personality to speak of.

We all know people who just love to talk, and very eloquent they may be, but they still couldn't sell water to a thirsty man without being shown how. No one is born with a natural ability to cut hair, fix a car, or lay bricks; they have to be shown how to by being trained or through real working experience. Just because your father was an engineer doesn't mean that you will turn out to be one or even have the desire to become one. You can be anything you want to be, if you put your mind to it, receive the proper training and are enthusiastic about that career path. Sales is no exception. So, if you have ever been told that you need the "gift of the gab" to work in sales, pay no attention.

In fact, the secret of success in sales isn't about talking alone; quite often it's more appropriate not to say a word when selling something. I've actually stood and watched people talk themselves into buying something, yet I've hardly said a word! Someone walking onto a used car lot, obviously wants or needs a car, and if they see a car that they really want, they will on occasion actually talk themselves into buying it — especially females, if it's a color they like!

Selling requires a good understanding of people and their everyday behavior, something we can all learn to a certain degree with a little help.

Most of us are naturally suspicious of salespeople by nature, and, as an example of this, what do you think would happen if someone came either to your front door or office clutching a fist full of money and told you that they had FREE MONEY for you? There you are, looking at someone waving a lot of bills in front of you and saying "you can have it all for free."

So what would you do, just take it? In the circumstances, it's very unlikely; chances are that you will be very highly suspicious and wonder to yourself "what the catch is." After all, you get nothing for free in this world, do you?

My point in using this example is to show that we, as people, tend to become suspicious or guarded towards others at the drop of a hat, even someone giving away free money. Therefore, it's important to have a basic understanding of human behavior and utilize aspects of this to your advantage when selling.

Everyday Psychology

As an example of how psychology can work for you, think about this scenario: You call at someone's door, and mum or dad answers with a young child attached to their ankles.

You naturally ask the child in your cutest voice "Hello, and what's your name?" remembering to keep regular eye contact and a nice smile with mum or dad as well, then go on to say "And how old are you?" Mum or dad will almost always answer for the child, if he/she is particularly young — "Oh that's Tommy, he's four."

You look straight at mum or dad and say, "Four, wow…he's going to be a boxer when he gets older."

Watch mum or dad's reaction, their chest just bursting out with pride. At this point, you're their new best friend! If it's a girl, you can replace boxer with ballerina; it works just the same. Before you know it, you will be invited in for a tea or coffee, done deal.

If and when you do encounter young children, it's always a good idea to bend your knees to lower yourself down to the child's height when you are talking to them. Otherwise, you may well scare them, and the last thing you want is to try and keep the attention of a parent who is trying to comfort a crying child. Remember, if there's a pet as well, the more the merrier…make friends with Fido, too.

The principles are the same regardless of what you sell or where. Be friendly, use psychology to your advantage, ask the right questions, listen, anticipate objections, and be ready to overcome any possible objections.

Using psychology to sell isn't something new, everyone uses it — just take a look at your local superstore as one typical example.

Those candies aren't at the checkout because there wasn't room for them within the main store. They know that mum or dad may well have the kids in tow and they will have to spend some "static" time at the checkout loading groceries. The store also knows that the kids will in all probability create a fuss to get some candy, that's why they are there, and mum or dad will buy some just to keep the kids quiet for a bit longer!

Supermarkets have the psychology of sales down to a fine art. How many times have you popped in to your local supermarket because you simply needed to pick up a carton of milk on the way home, and in the end you came out of the store with things you had no intention of buying?

Was it that wonderful and deliberate aroma of freshly baked bread that perhaps influenced your decision to buy that cake or crusty loaf of bread? Have you also noticed how all the brand name and subsequently more expensive items are all placed at eye level and within easy reach? To select that lower-priced identical item requires you to physically bend or reach. It's not just by accident that these things are displayed this way. Everything is carefully planned within the store so that you will spend more than you intended to; it's psychology in sales at its best.

We have all seen those food products that are advertised as being 95% fat free, haven't we? This reverse-psychology technique automatically gives the consumer the impression that it must be healthy or good for them. What the advertiser is actually saying is that their food product contains 95% other ingredients and 5% fat!

Would we buy something that was advertised as "New Splat Bar — CONTAINS 5% FAT"? In all probability we wouldn't buy something that told us the direct truth.

Of course, these are only minor examples of how psychology is utilized in sales. Everyone does it, even your local shoe store. "Buy one pair — get the second pair half price" is a usual sales ploy. You only went in for one pair of shoes, but came out with two pairs as such a bargain was hard to resist. In the process, you've spent more than you initially intended to or could really afford, and now you have another pair of shoes that you probably didn't even need, plus expensive shoe-care products you probably didn't want or need — but, hey, those shoes were such a bargain!

Have you ever asked yourself why gas stations sell you gas by the litre and not by the gallon? Yes, you guessed correctly, it's more appealing to see a low price on the billboards. You would have to do some mental math to work out the true "gallon" cost, but how often do you attempt to calculate the cost per gallon when your filling your car up? Probably never if you are like most people, who can't be bothered and simply look at the total display on the pump as they are filling up, not at how many litres/gallons they are actually getting for their money.

All retailers want you to spend more than you intended, and, what's more, you probably talk yourself into doing it, not the sales staff who usually spends their sales energy pushing the usually expensive after-care products or insurance cover.

Imagine this, you've just spent $900 on an expensive, quality, brand-name TV which the salesperson spent ages raving about. All of a sudden, as you're paying for your new pride and joy, you are asked if you want to take out extended repair insurance.

Think about this for a moment! The sales staff is basically telling you that you've just possibly wasted $900 of your hard-earned cash, and chances are you will be forking out even more money in the future for unknown, yet expensive repairs. They have succeeded in placing doubt in your mind about their own product's reliability with the use of a few choice words, but for the "peace of mind" insurance offers, you end up paying them more in repair insurance that it probably would ever cost should it actually need repaired! So you end up paying $1050 for a $900 TV that in all probability won't ever go seriously wrong!

When I'm in such a situation, as a consumer, I always respond to their seed planting by asking them "So what you're really telling me is that this product is no good?" They usually end up contradicting themselves all of a sudden by saying something along the lines of "Oh, no, not at all, this is one of our most reliable products." Then why do I need insurance? As you can imagine, a salesperson trying to sell to another salesperson usually ends up in a battle of wills. Most stores are glad to see the back of me!

Can you imagine being asked at the supermarket checkout if you wanted to insure those eggs? After all, they may crack or break on the way home. So, it's an extreme example, but the principles remain the same, and I've no doubt some people could be tempted to take out a policy on eggs that in all essence is useless; it's all about building value and highlighting the benefits of such a policy in the mind of the prospect.

People fall for these psychological ploys every day of the year. After-sales product insurance is big money and it's usually where the retail salesperson earns their main commissions. All they had to do was plant a single seed of doubt in the prospect's mind and then let the prospect's own imagination do the real sales work for them. This is something you can actually learn from and, in the next chapters, I will show you how to ask the right questions.

Building Values

No matter what sales market you are in, be it retail sales, door to door or business to business, you must identify the values and benefits of the product or service you are offering. This is the first essential step in creating the want and desire in the prospect for your product/service.

A common mistake salespeople make is to try and sell to the prospect using the benefits of their product alone. A benefit and a value are two totally separate things. The dictionary defines the word **value** as: *a fair return or equivalent in goods, services, or money for something exchanged: the monetary worth of something: marketable price.* Whereas the word **benefit** is defined as: *an act of kindness: **BENEFACTION:** something that promotes well-being: **ADVANTAGE**: useful aid.*

The benefit of a lease vehicle, for example, is that the prospect will be able to drive to their destination, not walk. They will also benefit from being able to drive a new car every three years if they so wish, as well as, fit all the kids and the golf equipment in at the same time.

The values in leasing are: It's is an affordable and low cost way to drive a new vehicle; additional values could be not having to pay for any maintenance, the CD player, the low deposit needed, etc.

It is very important to take your time and identify every possible value/benefit that you product/service could offer. Look at every possible angle — what does it do, how does it do it, and, just as importantly, what can't it do?

Another example of a good product value is in a simple roller blind. What benefits/values come to mind when thinking about roller blinds? They block out the sunlight, are generally unobtrusive, usually very easy to operate, they come in all shapes, sizes and colors. An immediate and additional value comes to mind. If they block out sunlight, then it stands to reason that they will save the purchaser money, too. How?

Well, if the prospect happened to use an air conditioning unit to cool the room prior to buying a roller blind, they wouldn't need to use it as much, if at all. Plus, if the blinds keep out sunlight/heat, they will also help reduce any heat loss through the window in the winter months, meaning lower bills all year round! What's more, the blind would stop furnishings/draperies, etc., from fading due to exposure to the sunlight, so these items would naturally have an extended life.

What values/benefits does your product or service offer the prospect and what needs will it fulfil?

(1) Is it the competitive price or build quality?

(2) Will it save the purchaser money or time; if so, how?

(3) How will it be used and by whom?

(4) What makes it unique, why should they buy it?

(5) Is it an improvement on something they perhaps already own or use?

(6) What does it do that your competitors don't?

As another quick example of this, let's assume that you are asked to sell a new variety of grass seed and after some thought you have managed to identify four initial values / benefits that your grass seed has to offer the prospect...

(1) It grows to be much greener than any other grass presently on the market *(value)*.

(2) It grows much slower than other brands on the market *(benefit)*.

(3) It's a special sow-and-forget brand *(value)*.

(4) Unusually for grass seed, birds can't eat this brand *(value)*.

We can then convert these values/benefits into some "keyword" selling points your grass seed has over other brands on the market:

(1) As this brand of grass grows slowly, it won't need cut as much. This is a major selling value/benefit, as it would obviously save the customer time and money in the long term, especially if they use a gasoline-driven mower. So the value is: *It will eventually pay for itself as they will use less gas!*

(2) The fact that it is a sow-and-forget brand, plus birds can't eat it, is another time and money saver for the prospect. Another value*: No more reseeding areas the birds have feasted on and no bald areas to worry about.*

(3) Being greener, the prospect's lawn will always look more luscious than the neighbors'... *eye appeal.*

Take a good, long, hard look at what you are selling and identify every possible value and benefit it has to offer your prospect and write these down. It may be worthwhile to ask a family member or colleague to do the same thing for you and compare notes. People often see things differently and, as such, having another view on your product's values/benefits can be invaluable, as they may well spot something you missed.

Therefore, when we come to creating our script, we can include these main points: Money saving, time saving, looks good, and pays for itself. So these would become our main selling points when talking to our prospective customer. We could therefore include some or all of the following statements/questions in our main sales script:

(1) "Have you ever heard the expression "The grass always looks greener on the other side of the fence"?Well, our grass really is greener!"

(2)" What kind of mower are you using at the moment? Is it gas or electric powered?" E*ither way, they will save money.*

(3)"How much do you reckon you spend on gas/electric each year just to mow the lawn?"

(4) "How often do you actually cut the grass?"

(5) "How much time does it take you?"

(6) "Would you like to reduce the amount of time and money you have to spend cutting the grass?"

Scripts, which I discuss in more detail later in this book, are important regardless of what you are selling, so for now think of what kind of leading statements or questions you could ask your prospect — using some or all of the values/benefits you identify about your own product or service.

Wherever possible, you should also attempt to build upon the values and benefits you have managed to identify. To do this really depends on your product or service, but for example if you are selling advertising space to restaurants in your area, you could add value to your publications credibility by telling the restaurant that in order for you to even consider carrying their advertisement, they would have to pass a strict kitchen inspection or perhaps an undercover food tasting. After all, you don't advertise just any old restaurant do you? In truth, you probably would, but they don't know that, do they?

This sort of approach has a very positive effect, not only on your sales levels, but for the restaurant. Instead of them looking at your publication as just another expensive advertisement, they will see it as an achievement — all because of the perceived credibility your advert offers them, as they had to pass a test. Before you know it, restaurants will be knocking on your door looking for space.

What Will it Cost?

Now that you've taken the time to list your product/service's values and benefits, you need to know how much it will eventually cost the prospect to buy. This is usually the main objection salespeople hear and, as such, you should always look for a value/benefit in your product/service that will reverse the perceived cost hurdle in your prospect's mind. As in the previous example, the response to any expected "cost objection" for the roller blind could be overcome with the value, that the blinds would actually save the prospect money and pay for themselves.

Either way, you still need to know how much your product/service will cost the prospects, so write this total cost down, then break the figure down into a weekly figure:

Product cost = $1000
52 weeks = $19.23 a week
Now break it down to a daily figure:
$19.23 divided by 7 days = $2.75 per day

Memorize the figures your product breaks down to. If you're offering finance, what's the lowest possible repayment amount you can offer? The reasons for this are simple; when the customer asks what the cost of your product or service is you can say, "It works out at less than $3.00 a day, the price of a good cup of coffee." This is much more acceptable to the prospect than saying, "A thousand dollars."

For the grass seed I used as a previous example, the final cost would naturally be determined by the area the prospect wanted grass to cover. Always give the positive response where your product would otherwise sound expensive. "We could seed that area for less than $4.00 per square foot." Never mind the fact they may want 400 square feet covered; it initially sounds much more acceptable to the prospect than saying, "That would cost $1,600."

Most salesmen of high-value products always break the cost down to its minimum level, including car salesmen. The prospect will no doubt see the listed price of, say, $16,000 on the vehicle's window, but the salesman is always quick to point out that the prospect could have the car for less than $200 a month or for $25 per week.

Breaking costs down into manageable chunks is more likely to keep your prospect's interest and not scare them from talking to you some more and allowing you to close the sale. Personally, when I'm asked by a prospect, "So how much will it cost me" or "how much is it?" I would actually respond by asking them, "How much do you think it would be?" Don't be afraid to answer a question with a question of your own.

This way you can determine whether or not you are both on the same playing field, and, if your prospect responds with a higher figure (which does actually happen on occasion — it all depends on how well you've highlighted the values to them), you could always say, "Well, you obviously have an eye for quality, but if I were to tell you that I can do it for you right now for only [lowest price figure] would we have a deal?"

What can they say? They've identified the values and given you a higher than expected price and you have just surprised them at just how affordable it is, so now attempt to close the sale by saying, "Ok, so shall we get the paperwork out of the way then?"

Should they, however, come back with a lower figure than the true cost, you could say humorously, "Well you're obviously a bargain hunter. You're well away from the figure I had in mind [true figure, but inflated by at least 10%], but let's see what I can do for you." Then jot down some meaningless figures whilst staying silent and try to look as though you are really concentrating too. Silence is golden!

At this point, if it is a couple you were talking to, they would look expectantly at each other in silence, then you can say, "Ok, here's what I can do for you, but don't mention this to the neighbors whatever you do." Now they automatically think the neighbor may have the same thing, but has no doubt paid more than they are going to get it for!

"Right, you already know how much this product will help you, you're good people, so here's the deal, you give me your order today and agree to say nothing about it to anyone and I will give it to you for [*true cost, less inflated amount*]. I can't be any fairer than that. What do you say?"

Pause and look expectantly at the prospect. You've initially told them an inflated price and your quoted lower price now seems more reasonable to them, doesn't it? After all, who can resist a bargain, as it may now appear?

Chances are you will go on to get your order and the prospect will be thanking you for selling them something. They are happy, you're happy, the boss is happy, so where's the harm?

A lot of salespeople use ploys similar to this and get results. Some may even tell the prospect that they would have to call their boss to see if the price could be reduced. The salesperson would naturally ask the prospect, "Ok, if I call my boss and if I'm able to get you the kitchen you want at that price, would you place your order today? Naturally, I can't call him and ask him to reduce the price just for you if you're not going to take up the offer. I'd look like a fool, wouldn't I?"

Now the salesperson is giving the impression that he/she is doing the prospect a favor, and, at the same time, is forcing a positive direct buying signal from them.

Once the salesperson has assured the prospect that he will do everything he can to get them that kitchen at a good discount, he would then call the boss and plead for the discount using certain words during the conversation, such as, "They are such *nice people* and I *would really like to help them* get this kitchen." The salesperson would beg and plead on the prospect's behalf to get the discount on the price, but in all probability the salesperson isn't talking to the boss — only to themselves or the speaking clock service!

After a few moments of conversation with a few positive nods or thumbs-ups thrown in for good measure, the salesperson would hang up relieved and tell the prospect, "Ok, it's a deal. Let's get the paperwork done before he changes his mind" or "He won't give us it for the price you wanted, but he will do it for this price, which is really fair — he's never reduced prices before."

The prospect now naturally feels obliged to the salesperson for going out of his way just to save them some money and in all probability will give the order. If the salesperson has indeed discounted the price at all, he has probably just cut his own commission level — not the sale price.

Scripts

Most companies, large or small, usually issue their sales staff a sales script, but you may find your employer doesn't and relies upon your skills as a salesperson to make the sales for them unscripted.

I can't emphasize enough the importance of using a script. Everyone who is anyone uses scripts in everyday life — even the best man at a wedding uses a script before delivering a speech, as do all wise politicians, including the president. Never be tempted to try and sell without using a well thought-out sales script. When creating your script, make it as simple as possible, no matter the IQ of your potential customers. By assuming that everyone has the IQ of a turnip, you won't go far wrong. You may meet salespeople who claim not to use a script, as they "shoot from the hip" when dealing with prospects. A more appropriate term is "shoot from the lips" and these people will actually lose more sales each day because of this ignorant attitude than they will ever make.

Your script is basically a story about you, your company and your product. It is structured in such a way as to emphasize the values and benefits of your product to the prospect by simply asking questions that are worded in such a way as to identify/create a need, desire and subsequently a want for the product you are selling. If your script makes use of unique product features, make sure you explain their relevance in very basic, easy-to-understand terms. When designing your questions or statements, make use of the Who, What, When, Where, How, Are, Have words as well as the "Is" word wherever possible. For example, "Have you considered the savings?," "Is there any reason why?," "What budget are you working with?" and try to include your product values/benefits in your questions whenever you can.

It's important to "qualify" your prospect from the word go. You don't want to be wasting time trying to sell them something which they can't use. For example, *if you were selling digital telephones door to door, you would want to ensure that your prospect already has a phone line in place, wouldn't you?*

To reiterate the importance of using the "**Keep It Simple, Stupid**" rule, here is a true example of what can go wrong. One of the companies I worked for was a new telecom provider in the U.K. Prior to their launch, the telecom market was owned and monopolized by British Telecom, which was then in government control. The conservative government later privatized B.T and introduced de-regulation, which allowed other private companies to provide telecom services in competition with B.T. These new telecom companies still used the B.T network, which they rented. This basically meant that I was able to call upon people at home or work and offer them far cheaper telephone calls. The customer kept their existing phone number, same B.T line and, by using a simple device called a router, it allowed all of their telephone calls to be placed via the company I represented at a much cheaper rate. However, due to the then high cost of owning a B.T land-line telephone in the U.K, a lot of people decided to use mobile phones, which were actually much cheaper to use than B.T, as you only paid for your outgoing calls and had no expensive line rental, which B.T charged everyone.

As such, and to qualify customers, I had to know very quickly whether or not they had a B.T phone in the house. If they weren't existing B.T customers, I couldn't help them. So, after introducing myself, I would ask, "Tell me, do you have a B.T phone in the house?" to which they would usually reply "Yes" or "No." However, one person looked at me with a puzzled look upon his face and proceeded to ask me to "Hang on a minute." Off he went into the house and I could still hear what was going on inside as the door was still ajar. From my position, I could hear all sorts of weird noises, things being moved about and eventually him asking someone else in the house if they had a B.T phone. After a few minutes, he reappeared, looked me in the eye and said, "No, mate, but I've got a Panasonic and a Binatone phone." He had totally misunderstood what I had meant by asking him this qualifying question, and he had gone inside to look underneath every phone he owned to see if it said "B.T" anywhere. I quickly changed my opening question to "Are you a B.T customer?" after this encounter. So, no matter how simple you may think your script/questioning is, make sure it is idiot proof.

A typical script for a telemarketer may go something like this:

"Hello, my name's Alex and I'm calling from ABC Windows. How are you this evening?"

"I'm just calling to let you know about ABC's new range in replacement windows. Have you considered replacing any of those older windows in your home?"

Depending on the prospect's response to the question, the telemarketer knows which step they should proceed to in the script. If the caller said "Yes," as is hoped, the telemarketer would go to section two of the script, which may go something like this.

"You have? That's great, as we have a fantastic deal on at the moment whereby you can receive not only a free home survey and estimate, but we're also offering a 10% discount on any future purchases to those people who book a free home survey with us tonight. Would you like me to arrange a suitable time for that free survey with you right now?"

Section three would probably have the caller asking the prospect other questions, such as "do you believe that you will be replacing any windows in the near future?" and, if they are, the telemarketer can note this detail and call back nearer the expressed time or ideally lead the prospect back to section two, getting the appointment for the salesperson.

All sales scripts are worded to achieve a desired result, either a firm sale or an appointment for the salesperson and include questions which will ideally give a preempted response.

Note how my example made use of keyword values wherever possible. "Free," "Discount" and how the caller always ends with a leading question for the prospect to answer.

As I said earlier, not all companies issue scripts and, as such, you as the salesperson may have to create your own. This is fairly straightforward, but takes a bit of practice. It's rare to write a script that will work for you first time around.

To begin developing your script or sales pitch, look at the product values and benefits you have created and use these as your script-building tools. Next, you need to ask yourself who you intend to sell to — who will be interested in your product or service? Does it appeal to everyone, or is it a niche market, e.g. pensioners, teenagers, etc. Just as important, who are your competitors in the field? Learn everything you can about them and their products, pricing, quality, etc.

Call your competitors and pose as a customer. If you can, have one of their salespeople come to you and record their presentation on a discretely placed video or tape recorder. Forewarned is forearmed, and you will learn just what you're up against. If their script or pitch was really good, **use it** and change it slightly to suit your own product or service. "All's fair in love, war and sales."

Assuming that, for whatever reason, you aren't able to do this and need to write your own script, begin writing your script in exactly the same way as you would a story — it needs a beginning, content and an ending. Your script should be structured in such a way that your statements/questions lead the prospect on to the next level in the sales process, just like the earlier numbers game.

Take plenty of time over your own script, as it will pay for itself when you start making those calls. Your script should contain who you are, who you represent and what you are offering. Include as many keyword values as possible and remember those all-important questions throughout. Your questions should always be designed to exact a response from the prospect that can lead you onto the next sales step. "How are you" always gets a known response, that we can preempt as being "I'm ok thanks" or "Not so good," just as "Is there any reason why you wouldn't want to save some money?" What response could most people give to a question like that? After all, who in their right mind is going to say or admit that they don't want to save money — everyone does! Be clever in your choice of scripted questions and remember, at the end of the day, people can only agree or disagree with any question you ask.

Using the principles of our earlier numbers game, you now know that each and every sales presentation should be structured into steps, and, in this example script, I am attempting to sell replacement windows and have the prospect pay using optional financing, as I would get an additional commission payment. This scripted approach has 13 steps, but each selling situation is different and may contain more or less steps. Step one is designed to take me to step two and so on, until the close. Remember to try and keep your script as simple as possible, if you can say what you want to say in only five words, don't use 20.

A typical beginning may go something like this:

Step (1) — The Introduction.
"Hello, sorry to bother you, I'm James Johnston from Sisco Glazing Systems — have you heard of us?"
It's always a good idea to have your opening line end with a question. Most telemarketing companies end theirs with "and how are you?" This leads the prospect onto the next step in the sales script.
(Await reply)
Assuming they haven't heard of the company, follow this by asking another question related to your product. If they have heard of the company, I would have replaced "You haven't" with "You have, that's great."

(2) "You haven't? Tell me, have you ever considered modernizing any windows in the house?"

Await response and expect negative reply. This step will also qualify my prospect at an early stage so I can know whether they are in the market for my product. Note how I used the word "modernizing" not "replacement" as a value keyword. Reply with another qualifying question.

(3) "You haven't? Is there any particular reason for that?"
I will only know why they haven't by asking the prospect.
(Await response)

(4) "Oh, the cost puts you off," "Have you ever received a quotation?"
Now I know the reason and I now need to confirm if they have previously had a quote
(Await response)
"You haven't, but you just know it would be expensive. I think you may be pleasantly surprised at how little it would actually cost you. Tell you what, while I'm here, I'll do a free survey for you. There's no obligation and this way I can tell you exactly what sort of price you would be looking at."

By asking, I have discovered that the prospect simply assumed that it would be an expensive project and naturally I am attempting to give them a quotation. Note how I didn't "ask" if they wanted a quote. Instead, through making a positive statement, I told them I would do a free survey. If they had said that they did have a previous quote, I would go on to ask who it was from and find out why they didn't buy, etc.
(Await reply)
Assuming I was given the green light…
Prepare quote

(5) Present quote
"Well, Mr. Boggs, having looked at the windows, I think you will be pleasantly surprised at how little we can replace those windows for, but before I tell you, can I ask you a quick question? How much was your heating bill for last year?"

(Await response)

I have done my survey and prepared my price of $4500 but haven't mentioned it at this stage. Instead, I want to reinforce a value my product has to the prospect by having them give me a figure about something they probably haven't thought of before, and which, on the surface, has no relevance to what I'm selling. Note how I used the words "How little," not "How much" when I was referring to my product's cost.

(6) "Well, the reason I asked is that most people don't realize just how much heat is lost from their homes due to old windows. In fact, the average heat loss is 45%. Did you know that?"

(Await reply)

My product value is that less heat will escape from the house with the modern window system I'm selling, thus reducing the prospect's heating bills. The windows will also increase the property value. I'm getting them to identify these values for themselves, and to acknowledge my positive statements.

(7) Reply. "So you see, Mr. Bloggs, replacing your windows now will not only increase your property value, but will actually save you a lot of money in the long run. Based on last year's heating bill of $2000, you would save yourself $900 a year, which means that your replacement window cost of $4500 would actually pay for itself within five years. By replacing the windows sooner, rather than later, they will actually pay for themselves, wouldn't they?"

(Await reply)

I have told the prospect the cost of $4500 and am attempting to have them think of the positive value that they will save money, and they won't miss the money, as the windows will pay for themselves. Again, close the statement with a leading question, preferably one which has the prospect agreeing with you.

(8) You agree and what color of frame did you prefer — the natural wood effect or the plain cherry?"

(Await reply)

I'm confirming the prospect's own positive response that they would indeed pay for themselves, and I'm now attempting to close by asking a positive "are you buying" question.

(9) "The wood effect, good choice — and when would you ideally like us to begin the work? We can have it done on Monday or Thursday of next week."

(Await reply)

The prospect has made a positive "buying signal" to me by selecting their choice and by indicating a start date.

(10) Reply. "Ok. Mr. Bloggs, that's the wood effect frame and the office will confirm the start date for you within 24 hours. And how did you want to pay for them?"

(Await reply)

Reconfirming their response, and I am now leading up to the financing I want them to take.

(11) "Cash, that's great, but did I mention that we actually offer very competitive financing?" *(I know very well I didn't, I was just waiting for the right moment.)*

(Await reply)

They have offered me cash, I now want them to think about the value of paying through financing.

(12) "I didn't? Sorry about that, I did mean to. But basically our financing plan means that you could keep your money in the bank and you could always use the interest you get towards your repayments, which we can do for as little as $90 month. Is this something you would be interested in?"

(Await reply)

I am offering further positive statements to the prospect, low repayments, etc., and asking if they now want to do it via finance.

(13) "It is? Well, it does make more sense at the end of the day, doesn't it? I just need a few quick details from you and I will make all the final arrangements. So I don't have to ask you a lot of mundane questions, do you have your check book handy?"

I received the response I wanted, reinforced the wisdom of their decision and closed the deal. I obviously need banking details and the fastest way to do this is to copy the information down from their check book.

By using well thought-out questions, along with your product or service's values in your script, you will make your sales life so much easier. Think long and hard about the questions you know are relevant and that can lead onto the next step. What possible responses could you receive to your questions? What answers have you prepared to lead the prospect back on track?

Once you've drafted your script, test it, test it and test it again. How easy is it to memorize? Does it flow naturally? Is it conversational? Try your script out on a friend or family member and ask their opinion before using it for real. Once fine tuned, go out and try it in the field.

Direct selling is a tough training ground for any salesperson, but I personally feel it's the best training ground possible. No two individuals are the same and having doors closed in your face certainly makes you re-think your approach and your script content very quickly.

You will probably end up making running adjustments to your script as you go along, and eventually you will have tweaked it to the point where you're starting to get results. Scripts do evolve, and you will, in all probability, end up with something totally different from what you started out using, but you will have a better understanding of what objections different people may have had to your questions and what responses you can use to overcome them. As you've gathered by now, psychology plays a major part in getting those sales, and, in the next chapter, I will give you more in-depth examples that you can use to your benefit.

Here's another example of a script that is designed to sell a fictitious self-closing toilet seat. I've identified the values that I will include, along with the cost of the product before putting pen to paper. Regardless of what you are selling, the principles remain the same.

(1) Who will buy it? I assume females would more so than males.
(2) It's more hygienic, reduced hand contact.
(3) It's inexpensive.
(4) It's novel.
(5) It's automatic.
(6) It's easy to install.
(7) Stops the wife complaining.
(8) Makes life easier.
(9) It's very comfortable.
(10) It retails for $38.

"Hello, Mr. *(name from door)*, how are you this evening?"

(In all probability we can guess he or she will reply "I'm good, thank you")

"Oh that's good. By the way, my name's Alan from XYZ — have you heard of us?"

(Identify yourself and company ending with a leading question)

"You have? That's great, and so you know just what we do then?"

(Get them to think about your product/company, and again end with leading question)

"You don't? So you haven't heard about our latest product?"

(Why you're actually there, again worded as a question)

"Has your wife ever complained to you for forgetting to put the toilet seat down?"

(A good key value question)

"Yes, we are all guilty of it, aren't we? What would you say if I told you that I have something that is not only more hygienic, but would also stop your wife from ever complaining to you about this again?"

(Creating a little intrigue)

"It's a self-closing toilet seat, takes five minutes to install and you will never have to worry about closing the toilet seat again — it does it all automatically. It's a fantastic idea, isn't it?"

(Explain the product values and benefits, again ending with a leading question that gives a positive response)

"Tell you what, why don't we pop inside for a minute so you and your wife can see how it works?"

(Getting inside with positive statement, and I would probably begin wiping my feet on the door mat as I was saying this)

(Spoke to and demonstrated the seat to both parties)

"So, there you are. It's really easy to install, self closing, much more hygienic than present toilet seats on the market and really comfortable. What's more, we have a choice of 3 colors: white, red and green. What color would you choose?"

(Reinforcing values and getting onto the subject to give you a positive buying signal by asking what color they would like)

"White? That's a popular choice as it matches everything."

(They have made a buying signal and I have complimented their choice)

"How many bathrooms do you have in the house?"
(Just in case they have more than one)
"So you would only want one then?"
(Reconfirming buying signal)
"And how would you like to pay? We take cash or major credit card."
(Asking for the sale to be closed and waiting for them to ask the actual price)
"Believe it or not, it's on special today for $38 and comes complete with the manufacturer's five-year guarantee. It's a bargain, isn't it?"
(Giving price, ending with further positive statement question)
"So how did you want to pay for it?"
(Attempting a final close. If it were an item that had to be ordered, I would probably be asking this question whilst holding pen to order paper)

Let's face it. You as the salesperson have to convince someone that they need your product or service and that they simply can't live without it, but the consumers have managed without it in their lives so far, haven't they?!

As I've stated, we use psychology each and every day, often subconsciously. We all meet different people every day and we instantly categorize them accordingly, don't we? Do we like them? Do they have money? Are they successful? Are they intelligent?, etc.

We all pigeon hole or categorize people within moments of meeting them based on appearance, manner, etc. I don't for one second class myself as a psychologist, but I do know people very well—just as much as you do in fact.

A good salesperson has many personalities. No. I don't mean we are all two faced. We just know how to carry ourselves in different situations and with different personalities and characters.

When in Rome, do as the Romans do — wear the hat that suits the situation and surroundings, including the company.

Here I will give you an example of how to use psychology to **your** benefit. Assume you're at someone's door, selling my imaginary product — the Super Dooper Pooper Scooper! You're dressed accordingly and the home you're calling at is very up-market — long driveway, rolling lawns and a gleaming Rolls Royce car in the drive.

The door is opened by a rather gruff-looking gentleman, who's obviously just had a hard day on the golf course.

> Man: "What?"
> You: "Hello, I'm Joe Bloggs from Super Dooper Pooper Scooper, how are you?"
> Man: "I'm ok. What do you want?"
> You: "I'm here to show you our new Pooper Scooper."
> Man: "Sorry, but I don't have the time" or "I'm not interested" *(assume door is closed in your face)*

So what did I do wrong?

Simple. I tried to sell my product straight away. But wasn't that the whole reason I called upon him, to sell my Pooper Scooper?

Let's look at it another way. You're in a nice restaurant for dinner — do you dive straight into the main course or do you start with an aperitif?

The same principle applies in sales — starter, main course and dessert (closing the deal).

Ok, so let's go back to Mr. Gruff with the nice big house and try a different approach.

> Man: "What?"
> You: "Hello, sorry to disturb you. I'm Joe Bloggs from Super Dooper Pooper Scooper. How are you?"
> Man: "I'm ok, thanks. What do you want?"
> You: "I like the car in the drive, is it yours?"
> Man: "Yes." *(Pleased that you commented on his pride and joy)*
> You: "Must have been very expensive."
> Man: "Yes, 300K."
> You: "Wow, but worth every penny I bet."
> Man: "Oh, yes, it does this, that and even makes the coffee blah blah."

The whole point is to initially engage your prospect in conversation, preferably about them or something they own. It could be as simple as a flower in the garden. Even if you aren't interested in it, feign interest. Listen, compliment, etc. People love to talk about themselves or their possessions — use this fact to its fullest.

You are well aware of what people think of us for disturbing their peace and quiet. You also know that when they have opened the door to you, they already have an excuse for not talking to you, so use a distraction technique like conversation before using your main script. There they are, just waiting for you to introduce yourself and start your pitch, when all of a sudden, instead of you trying to sell them something, you're complimenting them on their car or nice garden. This throws them right away and instead of saying to you "I don't have time," they are forced to forget that thought and reply to your unexpected comment.

"Oh, hi there, I love the way you've got the garden."

Having not expected this approach, they will naturally be thrown for a few seconds and instead of telling you "Sorry, but I'm on the phone" or "I was just getting into the bath," they will have no option but to respond to your nice comment about the garden. So, you see the importance of conversation and relaxing the prospect from the moment they open the door to you.

During this initial conversational period, you will observe a dramatic change in your prospect's body language. They will very quickly become much more relaxed and therefore unguarded, which is what you want. Once you've relaxed the prospect enough, move in with your main sales script, again using conversation. When the prospect has fully opened the door and is more or less standing outside with you, is usually a good indication that you have succeeded in relaxing them, so now move onto your script.

> You: "I couldn't help but notice you had a dog."
>
> **TIP:** Always make friends with the prospect's dog/pet whenever you can. If the animal appears to like you, its owner will….trust me on this.
>
> Man: "Yes, he's a Biteyer Legoff, only one of 100 in the country."
>
> You: "Really!" Compliment, compliment. Make friends with the dog, pat/stroke it. Again, more conversation with your prospect that leads to your script.
>
> You: "Can I ask where you usually exercise him?"
>
> Man: "Oh at the park, twice a day."
>
> You: "He looks good for it too."
>
> You: "So how do you collect the waste? Do you use a bag at the moment or a scooper?"
>
> Man: "Oh, I use a bag." (If he replies, "Oh, I use a scooper," you would go on to say something like, "You do! That's good. What

kind is it?") and lead on to your main script.

You: "So you know how unpleasant a task it is, not to mention the possible health risks?"

Man: "Yes, it's not a very pleasant task and my poor back!"

You: "Oh, you've got a back problem?" *(Said sympathetically of course)*

You: "It must be difficult having to bend over. Have you ever seen a Super Dooper Pooper Scooper?"

Man: "No, what's that?"

You: "It's an amazing gadget that cleans up after your dog, and the best bit is you don't have to bend over to use it. Really clever, isn't it?" *(Naturally, if you have a demo version or presentation folder you would be using these props while reinforcing the values of your product)*

I'm sure I needn't go on any further. You get the idea — get the prospect's attention in a roundabout manner. Conversational scripts work wonders. Get the prospect to talk about themselves or something they own and listen to every response. Use positive body language, nod, laugh or smile where you feel it's relevant and keep good eye contact — I don't mean stare at the prospect as if he has two heads, but eye-to-eye contact is very important. Don't overdo it though or you will unwittingly scare him or her away in an instant.

Getting Inside and Etiquette

The next step is to ideally be invited into the house. You can do this in any number of ways. Once you've obtained the prospect's interest, relaxed them to the point where they are freely chatting to you, and you're on the sales script, simply ask them, "Would you mind if we perhaps went inside so that I can explain it to you in more detail? After all, we don't want the neighbors knowing your business, do we?" In other words, don't be afraid to ask to go inside. Most people will actually invite you inside once they trust you and you have aroused their curiosity.

TIP: As you're asking the question about entering the house, don't be afraid to start wiping your feet on the prospect's doormat — you will find in most cases that they will automatically stand aside and let you enter…be bold.

Only you and you alone can decide if you are comfortable entering someone's home. If in doubt, STAY OUT. If you are invited inside and you don't feel safe doing so, tell them, "Thanks very much, but I'm afraid it's company policy that I stay outside." Tell them, "It's a stupid rule, but, hey, rules are rules." Most people will understand and remain cooperative with you. If it's raining outside, stay in the hallway or entrance with the main door open slightly, and keep the prospect in front of you and the main door behind you at all times. You can always progress deeper into the home later if you feel it's safe to do so.

This rule applies whether you are male or female. A male entering a residence occupied by only one female is open to all sorts of dangers, just as female sales staff are. Remember, you don't know these people and whilst the vast majority of people are decent, law-abiding citizens, some are just plain nuts.

Once inside the property, ask if you should remove your shoes if you feel it's appropriate — e.g. light-colored carpeting or your feet are wet/muddy. Wait for the prospect to close the front door and allow them to guide you to the room they will use. Let them enter first, if you can, and remember to say thank you as you enter the room. If other people are in the room when you enter (e.g. the husband or kids), make sure you say hello and ask them how they are whilst smiling.

Now you want to quickly scan the room and position yourself at the best possible seat, which either places you directly beside your prospect(s) or at least facing towards them. Wait until you are invited to sit down and, when you do, don't sit right back on the chair. That's a definite no-no! Sit slightly forwards on the seat and lean slightly towards the prospect(s), place your opened folder on your knee(s). If the TV is on, don't be afraid to ask for it to be turned down or off. Most people will do this anyway without being asked.

Don't remove your coat or jacket, unless it has been raining and your coat is wet, and always ask permission before you do so, "Would you mind if I took my jacket off, I don't want to get your chair wet?" Otherwise, you will cause your prospect to become instantly re-guarded and uncomfortable with your presence. After all, who said you were staying for any length of time? This is the automatic impression that you will give the prospect. All the while, you've been chatting about whatever subject you chose and kept that nice smile.

Once the prospect(s) are seated, pick up on your sales script from where you left off outside — e.g. "As I was saying, we are offering a free quotation on windows. What windows were you thinking of replacing?" and take it from there.

So, by using initial distraction techniques, you will be able to engage your prospect in conversation and ultimately get inside the home. To reiterate just how well this works, consider this approach for a moment. I was once working a neighborhood in Aberdeen one evening, and, as I was attempting to give up smoking at the time, I would chew on gum between clients — besides, it stopped my mouth from going dry. I wouldn't chew gum directly in front of the prospects, of course, I would discreetly place the small piece of gum to the side of my mouth between the teeth and cheek area, which allowed me to talk freely.

However, on one occasion, I approached a door still chewing my gum, rang the bell and, as I heard the prospect approach their door, went to slip my gum into its usual hiding place. Just as the door was opened, I bit my cheek by accident. There I was, holding my cheek in pain in front of the prospect. I looked at the prospect, who was now looking at me with a concerned look (I was clearly in pain), and said somewhat laughingly that I had just bitten my cheek! We've all done it, haven't we? The prospect smiled back very sympathetically, and, obviously concerned for me, proceeded to invite me in for a drink of water, which I gratefully accepted.

To cut a long story short, I made my sale and thanked her for her kindness, but my mishap had worked very well for me in that my subject was distracted to the extent that she invited me in without even knowing who I was or why I was at her door. People are very considerate of others in most instances and like to help when they can, don't they?

I decided to try this little experiment again on a few occasions to see what would happen. The prospect opens the door to an apologetic someone who's obviously choking on something ("Hi there, *cough, cough, splutter*, sorry, *cough*, but I just swallowed a piece of chewing gum by accident"). The vast majority of people invited me in to get a drink of water to relieve my coughing/distress. However, one heartless person just stood there and waited to see if I was going to drop down dead, and on a couple of occasions I would be brought a drink at the door. Naturally, I would make a speedy recovery, apologize with some humor and get on with the job in hand.

You may think that such tactics are underhand, unprofessional or outright deceitful on my part, but the important point is to remember why I was at the door in the first place — to relax the prospect, get inside and make a sale, which I did with relative ease on most of the occasions I tried this experiment. Remember — nothing ventured, nothing gained!

Distraction techniques are used every day by salespeople, and they do no harm as long as they are not breaking some law or other, which I would never condone or take part in. Assume for a moment you're a self-employed roofer and you're driving around a neighborhood canvassing for business. You see a roof that really needs some attention, you pull up outside the house, knock on the door, clipboard in hand, ladder propped against the building. You've taken the occupant's last name from the name plate on the mail box and a woman answers. "Hello, Mrs. Bloggs. I'm Tony from ABC Roofs. I'm just here to do your free roof inspection."

Mrs. Bloggs will no doubt reply, "Roof inspection? What roof inspection?"

You, looking at your clipboard, say, "You booked a free inspection with us last week. I'm just here to do it for you."

Mrs. Bloggs will now go on to tell you that she never booked any such thing naturally.

You: "You're joking, not again! This is the fifth time this month I've had false calls. Someone obviously thinks this is a big joke."

If you do this well, Mrs. Bloggs will share your frustration and you will naturally say something like "Well, seeing as I've gone to the expense of being here, and the fact I did notice your roof may actually need attention on my way in, you may as well take advantage of the situation. It's a free service anyway."

Chances are, people being people and liking something for nothing, you would go on to get the work.

White lies, as I call them, can be acceptable in certain situations. As an additional example, you may find it easier to tell your prospect that you're "from customer services" to put them off the scent that you're actually a salesperson. Prospects will naturally reduce their guard a little and be more willing to listen to you. After all, you're not trying to sell them anything, are you? And the phrase "customer service" has a certain helpful authority to it.

The way to use this particular white lie depends entirely on your own product or service. An example of how you may use this in your script is by initially saying something like: "Hello, I'm Joe Bloggs, from customer services at ABC Glazing."

The prospect will naturally wonder what a customer services

representative from ABC could want with them.

> You: "I'm here about the letter we sent you a few weeks ago."
> *(Naturally, you know that no such letter exists, but they don't!)*
> Prospect: "Letter? I don't remember getting a letter."
> You: "Oh," *(looking puzzled)*, "that's strange. Maybe it was lost in the mail or maybe you threw it out by mistake."
> You: "We wondered why you didn't respond."
> The prospect's curiosity is now peaking — wondering what was in the letter and what they would have to respond to. They will naturally be puzzled and ask you this question — as such, be prepared for it.
> You: *(looking in your now opened folder)* "Hmm, it appears that you qualified for a large discount on our replacement windows — which I can see you may need. It was quite an offer, that's why I'm here. Is there any reason why you wouldn't want the discount?"

If, by chance, they were in the market for replacement windows, their ears would prick up at the sound of "qualify" and "large discount," therefore inviting you to tell them more.

If replacing windows in their home hadn't even crossed their minds, there's always the chance they would want to hear more, especially as you just told them they may actually need new windows, but don't say anything like that unless they really did clearly need them replaced. Also expect to be asked why they qualified for a discount and have a reply to hand — "Oh, it was a random drawing done by zip code and yours was a winner."

Naturally, this is only one example of how white lies can get your prospect's immediate attention without them becoming overly suspicious that you're actually a salesperson.

A further example of this customer service approach was used very successfully by one electricity supplier in the U.K. Following the deregulation of the U.K.'s energy markets, consumers were able to choose whoever they wanted for the supply of both natural gas and electricity. In some instances, it was actually beneficial to the consumer to buy their gas from the hydro company and the electricity from the gas company. All very confusing for the consumer, but those that did this, actually did save a lot of money each year. One hydro company I worked with briefly decided to dress their sales staff in the same uniforms as were used by their own meter readers.

The sales staff would use a script that introduced them as being from customer services and would go on to say that the customer appeared to qualify for a discount on their gas and hydro, that they hadn't responded to their letters (which didn't exist), and was there any reason why they didn't want the discount?

This approach had great success as the customers, upon opening their front doors, would see what they believed to be a meter reader and promptly invite them inside to show them where the electricity meter was. The sales representative would, of course, allow themselves to be taken into the house and at that point explain that they weren't there to read the meter, they were actually from customer services and would proceed with their sales script.

This approach to sales may well shock you, as it would many people should they discover the truth behind this meter reader approach. However, it did work very well, as it relaxed the prospect and caught them off guard.

As the salesperson, it's important for you to control the situation. Ask the right questions in your script and you will get the expected answer. At the end of the day, people can only answer yes or no to your questions, that's if they are thought out properly and you, of course, will have the response(s) to your statement/question prepared.

Listening and hearing are two separate things, as you know. We all hear, but how often do we really listen? As a rule, when you're actually getting down to selling your product, you should be talking about 20% of the time and listening for the other 80%. You need to listen for those important buying signals which your scripted questions should generate.

For example, imagine you're selling satellite TV and your prospect's property has no visible dish. During your initial conversation, you can try and determine if they perhaps use cable. If they don't, great; if they do, no problem. If they have no cable service, they may only have a handful of stations — you will only find out by asking.

Your satellite system offers 300+ channels, and, even if they do use cable TV, you've identified they are familiar with subscription TV services and you simply have to identify the values by asking questions such as: "So you have cable, that's great. Can I ask how many channels you're getting at the moment?"

You already know the answer if you've done your research, but you want the prospect to think about the answer for themselves. When they reply, you would move onto your next scripted question: "40 channels, that's not bad. How much is that costing you a month?"

Again, you may well know the answer beforehand and have the next response to hand: "What would you say if I told you we offer 300+ channels for a similar price?"

Your satellite system may in actual fact cost more than they are presently paying each month at the moment, but you should go on to get the prospect to identify the true cost of their existing service for themselves. To do this, highlight additional values in your product by using those all-important leading questions, such as:

(1) Do you buy a daily newspaper? *(Who doesn't?)*

(2) Do you ever rent a movie for yourself or the kids? *(Again, who doesn't at some point?)*

(3) How often do you rent movies?

By asking such questions, you will get the prospect to think about something they probably never would think about normally. How many of us really think about how much we spend a week on newspapers or rental movies?

To close the sale, reiterate the costs the prospect himself came up with:

"So you're actually spending $30 a month for 40 channels of TV, $20 on movies and $25 on newspapers. That's a total of $75 every month, isn't it? What would you say to having 300+ channels, all the latest movies, no more line ups in the video store, and instead of reading about the news after it happens, you can watch it as it happens — for only $40 a month? That's saving you $35 a month, isn't it?"

Instead of you costing them money (which you are), the prospect will only see that you are not only saving them money, but giving them a better variety of stations and no more inconvenient trips to the video store. This is why identifying every possible value and benefit that your product has to offer is so important.

Whatever market you're in, do your homework! Who is the competition? What do they offer? How much do they charge? And remember to compare your product to theirs. If you look hard enough, you will find those key selling points. Product value is in the eye of the beholder — build upon it.

It really is up to you as the salesperson to create the need and want within your prospect as best you can, and, hopefully, you now have a better understanding of how this can be done, simply by giving thought to what you are going to say or ask within your script.

Handle Objections

Objections are simply people's negative, unwanted or unexpected responses to your scripted questions. People hate being sold to. They prefer buying something they need, and it is up to you to create that need within them, simply by asking the right questions. From my own experience, any unexpected objection is often best met with a question of your own. If you encounter a lot of the same objections, it is usually a good sign that you've not highlighted your product values well enough in your sales script.

If the main objection is the price (you should always have a prepared response to a price objection), you will only know where the problem lies by asking the prospect. "Oh, so you feel it's a little over your budget? What sort of budget are you working with?" Once you have obtained a response, work with the prospect using only the difference in the asking price and the budgeted price (Budget $2,000/Retail $2800).

Open by agreeing sympathetically with the prospect on the extra amount that's needed to close the deal.

"Hmm. $800 does sound like a lot of money if you think about it. Then again, most things initially seem expensive these days, don't they?"

Now you want to lead them onto the value of peace of mind or whatever value you decide is appropriate.

"Tell me, if peace of mind was a physical item, what price would you put on it?" *(How can anyone put an actual price on peace of mind? It is a great question to use.)*

"At least you know that your $800 will not only get you something that meets your needs, but will give you complete peace of mind, something at the end of the day which you know is priceless. So you see, if you perhaps decide to buy something cheaper today, tomorrow it may actually cost you a lot more than $800 if it suddenly goes wrong, so given the peace of mind you will gain from our product, $800 doesn't seem that unreasonable, does it?"

If you do your preparations right, you shouldn't come across too many unexpected objections, and, if you do, then rethink your script. In most cases, you will find that people generally offer the same objections and, as such, you will soon build a good library of objection handlers into the script itself.

Common objections door-to-door salespeople come across include:

I'm too busy right now.

I'm not interested.

I've just run the bath.

I'm just on my way out.

I'm just having my dinner

I'm on night shift.

It's not my house.

My husband/wife makes all the decisions.

I'm on the telephone.

I never sign anything on the door step.

The list is pretty extensive, and, naturally, there isn't enough room for them all, but they all have one thing in common — more often than not it's a lie to get you off the doorstep. It's the same for business-to-business sales, except its unlikly the P.A. will say "sorry, he's in the bath," but they certainly will give you other excuses. When you do come across such immediate objections, don't be disheartened, but try to use the objection to your advantage. For example, the "It's not my house" routine can often be overcome by simply saying, "Oh, that's ok. I can talk to you." (They didn't expect that answer, did they?)

Just because it isn't their house doesn't mean you can't talk or sell to them. You could always arrange to call upon them at their own address or glean information from them about the real householder.

Should someone be having their dinner, apologize for disturbing and tell them that you will (*looking at your watch*) call back to them in an hour or so — if you have time. Don't tell them at this point why you called upon them. If they ask, just say as you are walking away, "It's something I think you will be interested in hearing" and leave it at that — GO. Until you return, the prospect's curiosity will be building as to what it could be about.

If someone is too busy, don't be afraid to ask when the best time would be to call back. Usually when you do this, the prospect will ask you what it is you need to talk to them about. It's up to your own instincts to tell you if the prospect is telling the truth about being too busy or is in a suitable mood at this time for you to go into any detail.

If you feel they are being genuine about being busy and they do ask what you're calling about, just respond, "Oh, it's ok. I can see you're busy and I have an appointment to keep; it's probably best if I call back later, say around eight o'clock?" or whatever time you may choose.

The common "I never sign anything at the door step" objection, is in my own opinion best met with a humorously stated phrase such as, "That's ok, we could always go inside and do it." This usually raises a smile or laugh from the prospect. You can always follow this up with something like, "Why? What's the worst thing that could possibly happen?" then go on to reassure the prospect that they are not signing their lives away.

Objection handling, believe it or not, will become second nature to you given time. With experience, you will learn to handle the most common ones with ease. As I said earlier, each product will raise its own unique objections, and you should always try to anticipate these from your scripted questions. Before trying to sell the product or service, ask yourself why you wouldn't want to buy it; you will then have an idea of what possible objections you may encounter and can then adjust your script to suit.

So, in essence, the best way to overcome any objections is to try and anticipate what they might be and meet them head-on with either humor and/or a reverse question of your own. Oh, and don't forget the distraction routines I mentioned earlier.

Be Observant

As you approach a residence, you can instantly glean a lot of useful information about who resides within the property, including your prospect's last name, from the name plate or mail box. Is the property well maintained? Are the windows clean? Is the grass neatly cut or is it overgrown? Are there any children's toys evident in the driveway or garden? Is there a pram outside? Is there litter all over? Are there any signs that animals may be kept in the house, perhaps a warning sign or dog chain tied to a tree somewhere? Is there a vehicle or vehicles in the drive? If so, do they have child seats? What internal window coverings do they use? If it's net curtains, chances are it will be occupied by pensioners.

Look at your own neighborhood very closely. You will soon realize that most books **can**, in actual fact, be judged by their covers. Some people suit their pets, don't they? We all suit our homes; they immediately give a glimpse of our personalities and our characters.

Using the time it takes to walk up the path to the door wisely, can tell you what to expect when the door is opened. If they have children, you can even estimate the age range from the evidence you see lying around. This can save you a lot of time in the long run, as you will know if your product or service will be of particular use to the occupant before you even knock on the door. If you determine it won't be, you can always move on until you find a house that does meet your criteria. There's no point in you wasting time at a door that houses OAP's when you're selling some high-tech gadget aimed at teenagers. Use your selling time constructively. Saying that, however, there's no reason why you couldn't ask them if they have any grandchildren — there's always the chance grandma or grandpa would buy it as a gift for the grandkids.

One evening, I was cold calling at one door in Dundee and had ascertained that it was in all probability occupied by a pensioner; net curtains in the windows, nice border flowers and a generally neat garden. Sure enough, the door was slowly opened by a female pensioner, and, as I was going to begin my initial distraction chat, I was stopped dead in my tracks as I looked at her in the daylight.

My script was forgotten for a moment and my mouth was open yet nothing came out. There standing in front of me was this little old woman who had a beard and moustache some men would die for. I automatically did a double-take — "Yes, they're breasts, definitely a female" or was it some old transsexual? Do I call her/him Mrs. or Mr.? I quickly managed to regain my composure and continued, but I must admit I couldn't stop myself from looking at the hair on her face throughout…so always expect the unexpected. Some people have natural distraction techniques all of their own! I have even had an elderly gentleman open a door to me wearing nothing but an adult diaper, and, judging by the very strong aroma of ammonia that hit my poor nostrils when he first opened the door, it obviously hadn't been changed in quite some time. I apologized, said that I must have the wrong door, and it took a good few seconds for my eyes to stop streaming before I could move on to the next door in the street.

Door-to-Door Danger

I was once working in a very run-down area of Aberdeen in Scotland — an area I wouldn't normally walk into day or night, as it was extremely rough — even the dogs went about in gangs. But, on this occasion, my particular product appealed to low-income areas. Believe it or not, these areas usually have a higher disposable income level than some "better-off neighborhoods." A lot of unemployed people actually work illegally on a cash-in-hand basis, whilst still claiming all sorts of benefits, whilst those in the better-off areas are in debt up to their eyeballs to pay for the big house and fancy cars.

Anyway, I knocked a door in an apartment complex and a young man opened the door who appeared to be ever so slightly intoxicated, but nonetheless very coherent and friendly. He soon relaxed further and invited me in to finalize the deal I was offering. All I needed was a signature and a small financial deposit of five UK pounds. What they heck, he was friendly enough and being able to handle myself against such a small and unintimidating person, I entered the apartment, which was on the ground floor.

As soon as I entered the living room, I realized there was also another man in the room, and my eyes were instantly drawn to the disarray within, including drug paraphernalia on the table. I naturally said "hello" to him, slightly uncomfortable at this point, as it was very obvious that both men were under the influence of both alcohol and hard drugs, one much more so than the other. The second man's body language and tone of voice were very aggressive from the start and, by now, the person who had initially opened the door to me was standing beside the living room door, which was now firmly closed behind him. Talk about feeling trapped!

Natural instinct took over and I began to survey the room further, looking for another possible escape route if it were needed. The second man, who was physically much larger than me, began ranting to me about the prison he had just been released from and asked me over and over if I was a screw (meaning a police/prison officer). As the seconds went by, I began talking my way over to where the first man was standing by the door. The second man was now bragging about the fact that the man who had let me in was in actual fact his boyfriend and how people just don't understand their relationship. He proceeded to challenge me to give my views on their homosexual relationship, this was in between his aggressive outbursts, which I certainly was not getting into. In a matter of a few minutes, the situation just went from bad to worse and, knowing that there was no reasoning with them in their drug- and alcohol-induced state, I spotted my chance to leave as the first man moved to a table to pick up a can of beer and I beat a hasty retreat. Thankfully, the front door to the apartment was unlocked and I made my exit with what I could only describe as a cursing maniac at my heels. He had, somehow, in his drug- and alcohol-induced state, convinced himself that I was indeed a "screw." I dread to think what would have happened if the door had been locked behind me as I entered. He would have probably ripped my arm off and beat me to death with it! As it was, I thankfully managed to escape the apartment unscathed, with a complete screwball in a somewhat staggering, cursing and stumbling pursuit.

My point in telling you this story is that even seasoned professionals can and do get it wrong from time to time. You really never know what you're getting into when you're inside a stranger's home.

TIP: After this episode, I ensured that I placed the emergency services number onto one-touch number dialing on my mobile phone, something I would recommend to all door-to-door salespeople. It's very difficult to dial three simple digits if you're in danger or being pursued. So always think of safety — your own.

Animals are the most obvious danger for those working door to door, dogs especially. If the house you're calling at appears to have some vicious salesman-eating dog, and you're a little apprehensive about approaching the door, don't be afraid to ask the owner to remove the animal from the scene. Most pet owners are responsible and understand that some people are scared of dogs and they will usually be more than happy to oblige.

Speaking from my own experience, I find the smaller the dog, the greater the chance of being "nipped." Larger dogs are all talk — their barks tend to be worse than their bites. In most cases, a dog is simply letting its master know that there is a stranger around and, being pack animals, they are only protecting their family's territory. I was nipped only once in my own career by a little terrier dog and the owner was so apologetic it was almost funny. I will never know if they bought from me out a sense of guilt or whether they genuinely wanted what I was offering. So you see, every cloud does have a silver lining!

You will meet all sorts of people, as I've already stated, and you will probably see some sights that will make your toes curl, but keep a positive attitude and with time you will be hardened to most things. I've been offered everything from drugs to sexual favors in my door-to-door career (that's another book perhaps?) and there is every chance it will happen to you also. I must reiterate that what happened to me was rare — 99.99% of people are great fun to deal with.

Beat the Intercom

If you are working on a door-to-door basis for your employer, there is a high chance that you will come across buildings with security entry systems, usually in the form of an intercom system. It amazes me when salespeople automatically see such systems and, without even trying to gain entry to the building, simply pass it up as they think they will never get in. "He who dares wins," may be the motto of the British Special Air Service (SAS), but as the salesperson it should be yours also. Security intercoms, whilst a minor irritation, can usually be overcome by being bold and imaginative. The easiest way to gain access is to simply wait for someone to enter or leave the building and then calmly enter as they open the door. True, they don't know you, but chances are they don't know many people in their own building either. If challenged, you could always say who you represent and that you need to talk to some residents; then again, you could simply be visiting a friend or relative.

More often than not, I would simply press a lot of intercom buttons at the same time and wait. Believe it or not, some people don't even ask who is there and simply press the access button to let you in, but if this doesn't happen for you, simply say "can you let me in" to whoever replies.

If all else fails, pick an apartment at random and simply tell the occupant who you are and that you have been asked to drop off some information or to talk to them by your employer.

Making Your Mark

If you are working in a high-rise apartment complex, always carry a marker pen with you. The reason for the pen will become evident as soon as you start working. Each and every floor will, in all probability, look identical and it is very easy to lose track of who you have already made contact with. If it is an exceptionally large building, you won't be able to knock on every door in one shift, and will have to make a few return journeys and you will be glad you took that marker pen along.

TIP: When you knock on a door and there is no answer, place a discreet mark somewhere on or around the door frame and move onto another door. When you do eventually call back, you can see instantly who you haven't yet spoken with by the marks you have placed. As you go to re-knock a door, listen for signs of life inside and, when you are sure someone is going to answer the door, quickly place another mark next to the one you had placed earlier and put the pen away. Now you know that those people who you have made contact with will have either no mark on the door or two of them.

I would always recommend working large buildings from the top downwards, using the stairs to descend. Waiting for an elevator to arrive on each and every floor is very time consuming and as you are merely going down stairs, there is very little physical effort required. I've probably dotted thousands of doors in the past and can often imagine all these people one day discovering them with a puzzled look upon their faces as they ask themselves, "What the heck is that? How did that get there?" and subsequently sharing the story of the strange mark with a neighbor, who has also noticed strange markings on their own door. I expect that one day, I will read about a strange door-marking phenomena, that will probably be blamed on extra terrestrials in the newspapers. No doubt some UFO expert somewhere will be trying to figure out the "secret code" and why some doors have only one dot and others have two dots.

Referrals

Now, getting back to the subject in hand, I want to discuss with you the importance of referrals. Referrals are wonderful things and save you a lot of time and energy. Once you've closed your deal with the prospect, ALWAYS ask them if they know of anyone else who may be interested in your product/ service. Never walk away without asking for at least one referral.

Everyone knows someone somewhere and this is a powerful selling tool. Instead of you being a stranger turning up at someone's front door, you can relax the new referral very quickly by saying "Hello, are you Tom? I'm Joe

Bloggs from Super Dooper Pooper Scooper. Alan McBride suggested I call on you." Don't be afraid to use first names — it's less formal and I have never had anyone complain about me calling them by their name!

Your prospect will begin to relax and have some trust in you right away. You know their name and you've mentioned their friend's or relative's name, so you must be genuine and they will automatically drop their guard, but not their curiosity!

It's a great opener and if you use referrals as much as possible, your sales success will be much higher and you won't need as much leg work going door to door. At one point in my career, I did nothing but work on referrals, no cold calling at all. As I said, everyone knows someone — you get to know them too.

Curiosity

If you are working door to door, there is another piece of psychology I use to my advantage and that's people's natural curiosity. You probably know it by its other name — being nosey!

We are all naturally curious about our surroundings, what the neighbors have, how they afford it and this is something you can use as a salesperson to your advantage. If, for example, your product or service requires the prospect to sign a contract or some other purchase agreement, great! Make sure you print their name and address in nice bold letters.

Once you have your signed contract or agreement, you will naturally place it in your folder. Always place your completed agreements in such a way that when they have been folded, your prospect's name and address are clearly visible when your folder is re-opened. If it's your first deal of the day, place blank folded agreements behind the real completed one.

Why? As I said earlier, people are generally 'nosey' by nature and, when you call at the next house, have your folder opened, usually to the left-hand side of the prospect. This will allow the new prospect to stand alongside you and they will see your last client's name and address when they are looking at your brochure/pictures. As you are pointing to your pictures or whatever, stand close enough to the prospect and, again, at an angle that will let the prospect clearly see the completed deal you have in your folder….watch what they do.

As you are talking about your product and looking/pointing at your folder, you will gradually notice the prospect's head and neck slowly place themselves into a position that will enable them to discretely read the deal you just did, and they will also notice the thick bundle of blank agreements. The top one has a neighbor's name and address on it in nice bold print! You, of course, pretend not to see this maneuver and keep your attention on the right-hand side of the brochure/folder.

The prospect now thinks to themselves that, whatever it is you're selling, the entire street has it — except them! They don't know the contracts behind the completed one are blank though, do they? This maneuver really works wonders on a psychological level. They may not even fully know at this stage what it is you're offering them, but wow, whatever it is, a lot of people have got it, even the neighbor, so it must be a good deal.

We've all heard the expression "keeping up with Joneses." It's expressed because it's generally true. Most people do like to have what the neighbors have, or the same thing only much better or more expensive. Use this fact to your advantage at all times. I've even cheated and taken someone's last name from a door that gave no reply, then simply filled in the blank name and address portion of an agreement so that the next house I call at in the street will see the name and address portion. True, the prospect may know that the neighbor is out, but you could have called the night before for all they know.

Props

Props, as I call them, are good to use, as you can explain your product's benefits whilst showing them diagrams or pictures as you talk.

TIP: Even your ID card can be used as an ice-breaker prop — "Hi there. I'm Jim Craig from XYZ *(showing ID card to prospect)*. I have to wear this in case I forget who I am." This sort of approach usually raises a laugh straight away.

Most things can be classed as props, even the children, the pet, or the car in the drive, and, as I've explained earlier, these can be used to your advantage.

One very successful mobile phone salesman I know made millions of dollars in the early years of mobile phones. They were big bulky things at that time and still something of an expensive novelty. His sales approach consisted of him making an appointment with the prospect and, when his appointment time came, he would introduce himself to the prospect and, lo and behold, a couple of minutes later his mobile phone would start ringing. He would stop mid sentence and answer the call on its second ring. What the prospect didn't know is that he had arranged for someone to call him at that time, with instructions to let it ring twice then hang up. So there he was having a conversation with himself for a few moments before hanging up himself. He would naturally apologize for the interruption to the prospect. This was a very clever prop to use, as it demonstrated the versatility and convenience of mobile phones without him actually having to physically do much selling. He always left with an order and he later went on to open a large number of mobile phone stores in the UK, which he sold a few years later for fifty million UK pounds.

You have a vast array of props at your disposal, so use them whenever you can in your sales career.

Closing the Deal

There are many specialized books on the market about sales-closing techniques, but, to be truthful, closing isn't the most difficult thing in the world to do if your script presentation is right. You can't sell to all of the people all of the time, but you can sell to most of the people some of the time. Sometimes, no matter how good your sales presentation or script is, people just won't bite. Your product may well save them time and money, make their lives so much easier, but no matter what you say or do, they just won't buy. There are people in the world who just don't like change and are content with the devil they know, so don't get too despondent when you cross paths with them. You can lead a horse to water, but you can't force it to drink, no matter how hard you try. So keep closing in perspective; selling is a numbers game at the end of the day.

Knowing when to close your deal is really down to instinct and, of course, listening for those buying signals which your script should always generate. When you hear the prospect acknowledging the values of your product or service, this is usually indication enough for you to attempt a close. You very rarely close on the first attempt, so reinforce the main values that your prospect himself has acknowledged from your own line of questions, either verbally or through body language — e.g., nodding in agreement with you.

Believe it or not, a lot of salespeople don't get the sale simply because they never asked for it — ask and in all probability thou shalt receive.

"So you agree the Super Dooper Pooper Scooper will save you from having to bend over or hurting your back again? I'll just take some details from you and we can have it with you tomorrow," is one simple closing example.

"It's a great product, but they are selling really fast. I just need some details from you and I'll make sure you get one."

By making this kind of comment, the prospect is now under the impression that they may not in actual fact get one unless they act quickly and that you are perhaps doing them a favor. This forces them to make the decision to buy sooner rather than later.

Don't ever be afraid to ask for an order, but be wise with your choice of words. "Can I take your order?" may be to the point and may actually work in some instances, but I'd rather say something along the lines of "So, now that you've agreed it will help you, let's get the paperwork out of the way; it will only take a second."

As you're saying your closing line, take out the agreement form and place your pen on the paper in such a way as to give the impression that you're ready to begin completing the form. Remain silent for a moment, look at your prospect expectantly and, if no objections are heard in those few seconds, proceed to ask for their details. I have, on some occasions, depending on the sort of information that is required, had the prospect complete part of the form for things like bank details. It's a real put-off having to ask for their information line by line and this delay can give the prospect too much time to think; you don't want them changing their mind all of a sudden. So, if in doubt, have the prospect fill it out.

In some cases, depending on what you are selling, you may have to ask for a financial deposit. Obviously, depending on the amount required to make the deposit, you may on occasion come across the "I don't have my wallet/check book with me" objection. This is really frustrating; you've done your work and at the very last minute the prospect gets cold feet and gives you the above excuse. In this situation, tell the prospect, "Oh, that's ok (name)," extend your right hand to initiate a handshake, shake their hand and say, "Like me, I know you're a person of your word, so let's just shake on it for now and we will sort out the deposit later, ok?" The prospect will be left totally speechless and you will go on to get your deposit. They just shook your hand on it and who in this situation would want to say their word isn't good? Sneaky perhaps, but it works very well.

Get Their Autograph!

When it comes to obtaining a signature, never ask "Can you sign this now?" or "Can I have your signature?" The word *signature* can scare prospects in all sorts of ways. They automatically rethink their buying decision or assume that they are perhaps getting into something official that they can't get out off, and, at that stage, they may hesitate or begin to change their mind. As I have said throughout, people are strange creatures and can become guarded over the smallest things, like asking for a date of birth — especially older generation females!

Instead, ask them for their autograph and add, "It's just so we know you're over eighteen." Make a joke of it and remain light hearted. When you do need a date of birth, and, again, it's usually females who don't like to answer such a question, have them do it with the line "Can I just get you to pop your date of birth in this box for me? I guess they just want to make sure you're over eighteen"; most will oblige with a smile.

No matter who is completing the order form, be it you or the prospect, do whatever you can to get off the subject of the sale you have just made. Distraction is a salesman's friend and I would use it at this point in the transaction.

TIP: Have you perhaps noticed an unusual ornament or piece of furniture? Whatever it is, try and get your prospect to talk to you about it, perhaps about something you've read in the newspaper. "What do you make of that awful train crash last week" or "That's a smashing piece of furniture, is it an antique?"

Engage them in conversation and, before they know it, their mind's off the transaction they have just made and your agreement form will be completed in no time and safely tucked away in your folder. Keep some kind of conversation going until you're stepping out of the front door. Tell a joke if you have to, but keep it appropriate for the company you're in. Remember to say with a smile "Thanks a lot" and/or "Was really nice meeting you; thanks for the coffee" or whatever is appropriate. Silence may well be golden, but when it comes to form filling, keep the conservation going.

As I have mentioned earlier whilst discussing some of the psychology of sales, people like to talk about themselves, which is a fact a salesperson cannot ignore. It's not uncommon to visit people who are perhaps in the military, police, fire services, etc. Such people, usually without fail, have a photograph of themselves in uniform in some prominent place in the home or even the office — even if they have retired! These are gems to spot and use when you need a distraction or conversation piece, so use them whenever you see them. "Oh, were you in the army?" They will go on to tell you all about it, their adventures, etc. — be interested.

Importance of Being a Salesperson

Salespeople are judged by their peers and employers on the amount they sell, nothing else. It's common practice for employers to rotate their sales staff on a regular basis. Fresh blood is eager to please and will initially go all out to achieve high sales figures to please the boss.

However, the energy and effort required to sustain these high figures usually results in that salesperson burning themselves out and ultimately leaving or being fired, only to be replaced by fresh blood — and so the cycle goes on. It's important to ask yourself a few questions before taking any job offer, such as "Are the targets really achievable?" and, more importantly, "Can I sustain them day in, day out?"

What happens if you perhaps fail to meet your targets one particular month? Will you automatically be fired?

Seems harsh, I know, but a lot of companies really only care about the figures you bring in, not you or your well-being. Being part of a sales team brings its own additional pressures, as any good sales manager will publish your sales figures and those of your colleagues, which you will all get to see at your weekly sales meetings. The rational behind this practice is that seeing your name at the bottom will naturally make you strive to achieve more sales, but being at the top doesn't relieve the pressures as you may think. You will naturally want to try and stay there. However, such competition practices can also have a demoralizing effect, and it is the job of any good sales manager to recognize this possibility and to act upon it.

It seems bizarre that some companies should have such a cold attitude towards their sales staff and it's important to remind yourself that no one, and I mean no one, is more important than you and the job you fulfil. Companies may produce the goods or services in this world, but what would happen if they had no one to sell those goods or services?

You're the most important link in the production chain; without you and your selling skills and enthusiasm there wouldn't be any companies or corporations. Think about this fact for a moment.

Not only are you a salesperson, but people actually rely on *you*, not the CEO, for their jobs and this is why the reputation direct salespeople can often have frustrates me to no end. If anyone ever asks what you do for a living, don't just reply, "Oh, I'm in sales." Tell them you make sure everyone gets a wage. You're responsible for every person in your company. Without you no one would get paid each week, industry would collapse overnight, the economy would crash — the list goes on.

Being a salesperson is an honorable profession that offers you the freedom and autonomy to earn as much or as little as you want to, and the freedom to get out and about and meet new people every day. How many jobs offer this opportunity?

Positive Attitude

Positive mental attitude. We've all heard the term and this is something you will need at all times in sales. No matter how difficult it gets, no matter how many doors are closed in your face, you must stay positive. There are some people you just can't talk to in this world, no matter how gifted a salesperson you are. When a door is closed in your face or if someone is rude, it's only natural to want to call them everything under the sun — but don't.

A nice way to deal with such people is to smile and say "thank you for your time" — even if the door is half closed at this stage. So what, you're talking to a door, but they can still hear you inside. Being nice is the best way possible to deal with such people. It drives them nuts and most will feel guilty at some point. Sure, cuss them under your breath as you walk down the path, but do it **under your breath** and with a smile. Don't ever let one ignorant or rude person ruin your day or place negative thoughts in your head. Let one negative thought in and you are doomed. Negativity breeds negativity and before you know it you will have convinced yourself that you're no good, your product is rubbish and everyone hates you. Before you know it, you'll end up working at McDonald's cleaning tables.

Remember, the next door you call at may be opened by someone who has been waiting all their life for your service or product!

Ghosting

Ghosting is thankfully a rare occurrence, but it does happen. Usually this occurs when a salesperson, desperate to catch up on their colleagues' sales figures or realizing their days are numbered, decides to submit ghost deals. They usually do this by locating an empty or newly built property, taking a name from someone's door or voters role and completing the sales agreement form using that name and new address along with a forged signature.

They will then submit these ghost deals, take the commissions and run or pray that the company doesn't take steps to check them out in a hurry. Usually companies write to the ghost customer thanking them for their business or order and naturally the letter would arrive at an empty house. Even if someone had moved in, by the time the letter arrives, the occupants would assume it was meant for the previous occupant and return it to the mail service or, more often than not, put it in the bin.

Depending on the company's delivery times, they would usually only find out it was a ghost order when they attempt to make delivery or collect payment. Meanwhile, the rogue salesperson has moved on with his commission checks. Most companies are now aware of such schemes and, as such, have very good procedures in place to do follow-up checks, so never do it. You will be caught and, in all probability, arrested for fraud, but pressure to reach goals can do strange things to people.

Avoiding Pressure

One good way to avoid putting yourself under undue pressure is to hold back deals. Let's assume that your company expects you to do at least six deals per day to achieve your monthly sales target. Let's face it, we all have good days and bad days and on those good days you may sell more than six times. It's natural to want to go into the office the next morning to submit your bundles of sales agreements from the previous day or evening's work. Don't! And I'll explain why you shouldn't.

Submitting the ten deals you sold yesterday may well do wonders for your ego and put a smile on your boss's face, but by doing so you're actually adding to your own pressure. The next day you know you have to go out and achieve six more sales minimum and what happens when you have one of those bad days and only get two? You're four short and your previously inflated ego will take a dive when you have to submit only two deals to the office the next day — no pat on the back from the boss either!

The way I would avoid this situation would be to hold back a number of deals. Assuming I sold ten deals in one day instead of my targeted and expected six deals, I would hold back four of the deals by one day. When I submit my six deals, I'm happy and the boss is happy and I know that I'm not under as much pressure tomorrow, as all I now need to meet my target of six is two deals and, who knows, my bad day could be today. However, should I have another good day, I'd submit the four deals from the previous day along with two others to meet my target and hold back the rest and so on.

This practice is legal and harms no one. The company still gets all of my deals and I still meet or exceed my monthly targets and all this without any stress. You will actually perform better when you're relaxed and not under tremendous pressure to achieve for fear of losing your job.

Rogues

I have personally worked alongside people who class themselves as "professional salespeople," but who were actually nothing but rogues. Such salespeople jump from position to position, attracted usually by high commission levels and the chance to make a fast buck — they would sell their own mothers if they could for just for a few dollars!

These people give the true direct sales professionals a bad name. Just ask a friend of yours what their opinion is of used car salesmen or door-to-door salespeople. Most people simply don't trust them, which is a direct result of the quick buck rogue salesperson who doesn't believe in the product or service and will do or say just about anything to make a sale.

The vast majority of direct salespeople, however, are professional, reasonably honest and, as such, adhere to some sales ethics, something which brings its own additional rewards — repeat business or referrals.

The bottom line in direct selling is to be as honest as you can with your prospective client. Don't overinflate the product or service's ability to do something you know it can't just to close the sale. You will only be caught and the next direct salesperson to call at their door will bear the brunt — I guarantee it! It's a constant struggle for all salespeople; the pressure to meet your targets can at times seem overwhelming, and if you only need one more sale to meet your target, it's very tempting to inflate things to close a deal. Don't do it. That one inflated sale will in all probability come back to bite you when you least expect it.

Motivational Seminars

Have you seen advertisements for sales training courses or seminars and been tempted to attend them in the hope of obtaining sales tips or some formal sales qualification? Don't waste your time or money unless you know for a fact that you can really use what they will show you.

Such seminars, in all fairness to them, can be very entertaining, but again they all emphasize too much on motivation, and, by the time you get home, you have perhaps forgotten any real sales tips they did reveal, if any. You pay your money and make your choice, but at the end of the day you should remember that the only real sales certificate a salesperson should strive for *(and the only one that means anything to a prospective employer)* has dollar signs on it — your paycheck!

I personally keep my pay or commission statements and usually submit photocopies of the higher value ones along with my CV to prospective employers. This tactic usually gets the employer's attention very quickly, as it immediately proves that I can sell, unlike a sales certificate that merely shows I've completed a course in selling skills and, for which, in all probability, I paid for. Face it, who would you employ? The person with a fancy-sounding certificate in selling or the person with the paycheck showing commission of $20,000 for one month?

You Keep on Knocking but You Can't Get In

You've prepared a killer script, dressed accordingly and you can't wait to get out there and sell, sell, sell. So off you go in search of a suitable neighborhood in which to practice your craft. You approach your first door, know exactly what you're going to say when the door is opened. You ring the bell and wait…no answer. You ring the bell again, still no answer. Damn! No one is home. This goes on for the next 20 doors. By now you're feeling totally deflated — where the heck is everyone?

Timing is everything in door-to-door sales and I just don't mean your sales presentation. You have to remember that not many people are at home during the daylight hours and those who are at home are usually retired, unemployed, single parents or night-shift workers. Parents of school-age children will naturally not be at home until about 9:30 a.m., as they have had to drop the kids off at nursery or school first thing and will have to collect them again at either 3:00 - 3:30 p.m., so these times are "dead spots," as I call them.

Depending obviously on what you are selling and to whom, you have to think carefully about your working hours and adjust these to suit your target. To achieve the best possible number of hits, it's always best to work between 4:30 p.m. and no later than 8:45 p.m. Monday to Thursday. It's ok to work a little later on a Friday evening, say 9:00 p.m., as most people may not have work the next day and you will make more hits during these times. The more people you get to talk to the more likely you will get to sell, so think about your working hours carefully. Why spend ten hours knocking on doors and only getting to talk to a handful of people, when you can work half the time and talk to 10 or 20 times as many people?

Be sure to check with your local authorities, as they may have rules governing the times that people can work door to door and you may even need special permission. It never does any harm to visit the local police office of the neighborhood that you intend to work and identify yourself and the area you will be working. Should someone be suspicious of you and call the police, they can be reassured that you are genuine by the police officer.

Business-to-Business Sales Tips

Assuming that you are not working door to door, but perhaps in the business-to-business field, you may find these tips useful for getting an appointment with the prospect.

Gatekeepers, as they are referred to in the trade, come in all sorts of guises, but are mostly receptionists or personal assistants to the person you want to talk to. It is their job to shield all calls to your prospect and, as such, you should view the task of "making contact" the same way you would a game. You have to outwit these gatekeepers by any means possible to get through to your prospect, meet them face to face, and make your sale.

Naturally, you will want to know as much as you can about the company you're going to be selling to, as well as the person you want to contact. If it's a larger-sized business, chances are they will have an Internet presence — find out by searching the company name on the Internet.

Most websites are pretty informative and even allow you to email the company directly, perhaps your prospect's email address is listed. It's not usually a good idea to try and get an appointment by writing an email, chances are your prospect will get hundreds a day from people just like you and probably won't pay much attention to them. If you do decide to try this approach, you really have to make your email stand out from the rest by using your imagination. What will make them want to read your email? What will make it different from the many others they will receive each day?

One novel approach is to put the words "Bad News" on the subject line. More often than not, the prospect's curiosity will make them open it up; after all, bad news travels fast.

Hello (Prospect's Name),

Bad news travels fast, but news good or bad travels even faster now if you use ABC's fax machines. Did you know that our machines actually save businesses money by transmitting the data much faster than the system you're probably using just now? You could save up to 20% on your annual phone bill simply by using ABC machines.

Five minutes of your time could repay itself many times over, couldn't it? You have nothing to lose, lots to gain. Call me at 555-5555 any time to arrange a free demonstration.

Regards,
(Your first name and telephone number)

So, when it comes to emailing, be imaginative. You never know, your luck and chances are even; if they don't get back to you they will have at least heard of you.

The only sure way to stand a good chance is to meet them face to face, and, before you can do that, you have to talk to them, not the PA or receptionist. If you don't know the name or email address of the person who has the buying power, simply phone up the company and tell them "I've been asked to mail some information to whoever is responsible for buying photocopiers" or whatever it is you're selling. "Can you tell me who I should address it to?" You could always say in mid-sentence "Actually, I just had a thought, it would probably be quicker to email it over. What's (the prospect's) email address?"

Chances are you will get your prospect's name and email address, and don't forget to ask the name of the person you are presently talking to. It may come in useful later.

If, by chance, the gatekeeper refuses to give you the email address, but you really do need it, try this approach. Call back another day (about lunch time) and ask for the person you spoke to previously by name (gatekeeper). If they happen to be out for lunch there will be someone covering for them until they return.

"Oh, hello there, is Mary available? No...oh dear. Maybe you can help me. (Prospect's name) emailed me with some information and my computer crashed as it was coming in. Will you give me (prospect's name) email address so I can get back to him?"

Chances are you will be given the information you need as the stand-in receptionist would be under the impression that you know your prospect well; you even know Mary!

If Mary was to actually answer, there is nothing wrong with trying this approach; after all, it's unlikely that she will remember you out of all the calls she screens each day.

"Hello, Mary, how are you? (Prospect's first name) asked me to email some confidential information over to him, but I'm not at the office today so I'm going to use a remote computer station to send it. What's the email address again?"

Nothing ventured, nothing gained.

To get through to your prospect on the telephone, call up and say, "Hello, it's (your name). Can you put me through to (prospect's name)." If they ask you what it's regarding just say, "Oh, I'm afraid it's actually a private matter" or "It's about the letter (prospect's name) sent me last week" or "It's to discuss a letter/email (prospect's name) received."

By using a little imagination, and perhaps a few harmless white lies and some persistence, you will eventually get to talk directly to your prospect and hopefully go on to get your appointment. Again, use a well thought-out script to do this. Don't try to sell over the telephone. Design your script to get the prospect's initial attention and make the appointment from there — then you can make your sale face to face.

When your appointment time comes, be on time. If you are running late for whatever reason, even a few minutes, call ahead and tell them. There is nothing more aggravating to a prospect than a sales rep turning up late. It gives the wrong impression from the very start and chances are they may not see you or buy for this very reason. Petty but true!

When you do enter the office, it's not uncommon for the prospect to be seated behind a nice big desk with a few chairs placed in front of it. Naturally, you will extend a handshake and introduce yourself and wait to be seated. Believe it or not, some people actually make sure that these extra office chairs are lower than the one they will be sitting on.

This has an immediate psychological effect on anyone sitting on them. There you are looking up to your prospect and they are now looking down on you! Talk about feeling belittled.

When you do shake hands with your prospect, it is important to match grip for grip. So if their hand grip is say a little limp, keep yours the same; don't try to dominate the handshake. You may actually find some people, when they take your hand, grip it tightly and proceed to turn your hand so that theirs is on top of yours and your knuckles are pointing towards the floor; to me it's a primitive form of wrestling. These people are basically attempting to show you from the offset who is in charge; it is a poor psyhcological tactic that is supposed to place them in charge. Let them do it. Basically, they are generally weak individuals who are actually very insecure and use the office environment to "flex their muscles." In my own opinion, they are probably dominated at home by their partner. If such tactics will make them more relaxed, then let them think they are in control. In reality, you, as the salesperson, will be the one in control of the situation — not them. So when someone does this to you, simply picture them at home with an apron on doing the dishes with a nagging partner in the background.

Former US President Bill Clinton, like other statesmen, have the handshake down to a fine art. Next time you see a statesman on TV news at home, watch how they go about the business of shaking hands, something they probably have to do hundreds of times a week. Bill Clinton, as an example, would extend his right hand, grip the other person's right hand firmly, and using his free left hand, he would proceed to either momentarily grip or give a gentle tap just above the right elbow of the person he was shaking hands with. Try this for yourself and see what happens, but be sure to make it a smooth natural process as you are actually invading personal space. This maneuver, whilst small and perhaps insignificant to the unwise, is basically a way of saying, "Hey, I'm a nice guy, you can trust me and I really like you." And it works.

TIP: In every selling situation, you have to remove the obstacles in your way and that includes the office desk! Try not to sit opposite the prospect and talk over the desk. After you have been invited to take a seat, pick up or slide your chair to be next to them and say, "Actually, it's probably better if I sit next to you, that way you will have a better view of what I have here. You don't mind do you?"

How can they mind? You've already done it!

This maneuver actually places *you* in control, not them, by removing the obvious barrier between you both, and, believe it or not, you will both relax much faster than you would have done otherwise.

Be creative in your approach to selling at all times and, above all, relax and have fun. There are endless ways to get your hard-to-get-hold-of prospect's attention, whether it's by leaving your business card for the prospect's perusal with a small pack of candy attached to it and a note on the back saying "I've got a really sweet offer on at the moment, can I share it with you?" to sending a $1 lottery ticket saying "Odds may be 100 million to one of winning the jackpot, but I still gave you that one chance to win! Will you give me a chance?"

On the subject of business cards, I was once drafting a handwritten letter inside my car to a client thanking them for the meeting I had with them earlier that morning onto letter-headed stationary, which was the last one in my briefcase. Halfway through the letter, I couldn't for the life of me remember how to spell appreciate. Seems silly, I know, but for whatever reason my brain froze. Not wanting to misspell the word on my main letter, I took one of my business cards and wrote "appreciated" across the front. Satisfied with the spelling, I continued with my letter and without thought returned my business card to my wallet. A couple of days later on a cold call, I introduced myself to the prospect and handed him my business card, which he automatically looked at (we all do, before putting them away somewhere and forgetting about them).

As he looked at my card, he screwed his face up a little and said slowly to me, "Appreciated, why is that written on the front?"

I had completely forgotten about the "spell check" and was momentarily at a loss as to how I could explain my occasionally poor spelling skills. From out of nowhere, I replied, "Oh, I just wanted you to know how much I appreciated you sparing the time to see me today and that I also appreciated the opportunity to perhaps do business with you."

The prospect smiled back at me as though he were ten feet tall, put my card in his wallet, put his hand on my shoulder and led me into his office where I went onto getting an order. From that day on, I hand wrote in nice bold letters, "It's appreciated" across the front of all my business cards. Try it for yourself, it turned out to be one great icebreaker for me, and, because the card was a little different, it didn't end up in the bin or shoved to the back of a drawer, which is what happens to most business cards.

No matter what your approach is, make it unique and fun. There is no guarantee the prospect will see you, but they will certainly remember you when you call them and you have nothing to lose, but everything to gain.

One very little-known ploy is to find out what car your prospect drives. If you know what they look like, you may do this by simply waiting outside their office in the evening or early morning to see where they park or by simply asking someone who works there — perhaps a staff member outside having a cigarette. Again, a white lie may be needed — "Hi there, (prospect's name) wanted me to check out a scratch on his car door, but I forgot to ask where it was parked. Can you tell me which one it is?"

A lot of companies have reserved parking spaces, and, if you are lucky, your prospect's name or job title will be on one of these signs.

The next step is to leave a handwritten note on the windshield saying, "Hi, long time no see. Was passing and saw your car. Call me ASAP, have a great offer for you. (Your number.)"

What will hopefully happen next is the prospect will find the note, read it and begin asking themselves, who could it be? People being what they are — nosey — there is a very strong chance the prospect's curiosity will get to the point where they will, in actual fact, call the number to see who left the note. If and when they do call, they will naturally ask who they are talking to. You do the same thing — remember, you're not supposed to know their name at this stage, are you!

Once the names are exchanged, the prospect will be trying to recall anyone they know with your name and, at the same time, they will explain to you about the note they found on their car.

You act naturally embarrassed at the "genuine mistake" you must have made and have some fun with it, "I'm really sorry, (name). You see, I have a client that drives the same kind of car as you and the plates looked right. I thought you were him and, as I didn't have his number with me, I just wanted to tell him about a new fax machine that could save his company an absolute fortune each year. I don't suppose *you* know of anyone that would want to cut their business fax bills in half do you *(said jokingly, of course)*?"

The note is your distraction routine, which you use to lead the prospect into calling you, which then gives you valuable time to talk with them in a light-hearted and humourous manner. Hopefully, you can engage them in conversation that will allow you to again raise their curiosity a little further about your product. Depending on how well your staged conversation goes, there is nothing to stop you from popping in to see them; after all, the prospect will now know your name and you can tell the gatekeeper very matter of factly that "You spoke with (the prospect) last week and you now want to make an appointment to follow up on your conversation."

As I said, there is no end to the possible ploys and distraction techniques to help you meet your prospect face to face, so be imaginative and be bold.

Remember, just as with door-to-door sales, initial distraction techniques should be used and offices are usually full of them. Look for some conversation piece that may be on the desk or elsewhere within the office and use that to relax the prospect; i.e., A family photo or, better still, a child's drawing on the wall. A lot of parents with young children do take their children's artwork to display somewhere in the office. When you spot these, you can always say, "Oh, I see you have a budding artist in the family!" They will always respond with a big smile and go on to tell you all about the kid(s). Some will even show you photographs — make sure you always compliment the family pictures.

When making cold telephone calls to obtain appointments with prospective clients, having a script prepared in advance will make things much easier for you in the long run. Here is an example script, which can be modified to suit your own product or service, and which I have personally made use of with good results. Remember to smile and stay cheery when you are talking on the telephone; the prospect may not be able to see you physically, but they certainly can sense your mood very easily and will quickly build a rough mental picture of you in their heads.

You: "Hello, (Name). How are you today?"

You: "My name is (your first name) and I represent (company name), have you heard of us?"

Them: "Actually, I haven't."

Assume they haven't, but this lets you lead on to telling them what you do.

You: "We specialize in *(whatever you do or offer)* and what I would like to do today is arrange a ten-minute appointment to see (prospect's name), as I know they would really benefit by seeing what we can do for your company. Would you be kind enough to squeeze me in for ten minutes or less next Monday *(or whatever day you choose)*?"

Most, if not all, gatekeepers have a sense of "omniportance" and by briefly telling them what it is you do, you are including them in the process. You are also letting them know that their boss/ company may actually benefit simply by seeing you for ten minutes or less. You are also recognizing their position by asking "would you be kind enough."

By being upbeat, recognizing the position of the gatekeeper, and by simply using their name, chances are they will attempt to fit you in somewhere, so try and remain flexible when it comes to dates and times and, above all, be persistent. You, as the salesperson, are only limited in your abilities by your own imagination. Don't ever be afraid to try something new. Just because it's not been tried before, doesn't mean it won't work.

Let's Recap

To recap on what I have divulged, here is what you should do when working in direct sales and the principles remain the same for any selling situation.

(1) Know your product inside out, including the cost(s) and be enthusiastic about it.

(2) Know your competition as well as you know your own products.

(3) Prepare a script using simple, well thought-out questions that will elicit a positive response and lead the prospect on to the next stage. e.g. "Is there any reason why you wouldn't want to lower your telephone bill?"

(4) When approaching a residence, be observant and glean what information you can from what you see.

(5) If possible, get the prospect's name from the mail box or name plate.

(6) Knock the door firmly, or ring the door bell.

(7) As the door is being opened, SMILE.

(8) As soon as eye contact is made with the prospect, take one small deliberate step away from them.

(9) If possible, use an initial distraction technique. e.g "Oh, hi there, I really like the way you've got the garden" and be relaxed in your delivery.

(10) Engage in friendly conversation, remembering to smile and remain interested in what they have to say. If there is a family pet, make friends with it or the child(ren).

(11) At the correct moment, introduce who you are from. e.g "By the way, I'm from ABC windows," show them your ID card at the same time, if you have one, and make a joke. e.g "I have to wear this in case I forget who I am." Remember to smile/give a small laugh as you say this.

(12) Lead into your main script. e.g "Have you by any chance heard of us?"

Go on to explain what you are offering in the very simplest of terms. e.g "The reason I'm here is that we have a great offer on at the moment that will reduce your yearly heating bill by 45%, would you be interested in saving some money?" or "Is there any reason why you wouldn't want to reduce your heating costs?"

Remember, each question you ask should be designed to not only highlight your product values, but to also exact a response that will take them to the next level of the sales process.

(13) If you want to go inside, ask at the right time and slowly begin to wipe your feet if they have an external doormat and only if you are standing on it!

(14) Once inside, remember how to sit, what to look for and the correct etiquette to use.

(15) Once you have made the sale, get their autograph and again use a distraction.

(16) Ask for a referral.

(17) As you are leaving, thank them for their time.

You now have a great wealth of information to digest and subsequently implement into your own sales approach. All the information I have divulged in this book has been tried and tested in the field and has evolved through the wear of a lot of shoe leather. The tactics I use don't only work for me, they have worked with successful results for a great deal of people all from different backgrounds and who all offer different products and services. I'm confident that your own sales success will increase dramatically by utilizing some or all of what you may have learned, so good luck and I hope you will have a lot of fun in your career.

Thank you very much for buying my book and I wouldn't be much of a salesman if I didn't ask you for at least one referral, would I? Therefore, I would very much appreciate it if you could perhaps recommend this book to a colleague or friend directly, or perhaps you could email me with their name and email address at *sales_assistant@tiscali.co.uk* Please remember to include your own name & address, so that I may send you a personal thank you. Once again, thank you for choosing *Keep It Simple, Stupid* and happy selling.

Printed in the United Kingdom
by Lightning Source UK Ltd.
103012UKS00002B/43-78